I0020072

MASTERING SQL SERVER FOR

DATABASE ADMINISTRATORS

Proven Expert Strategies to Optimize, Secure, and
Manage High-Performance SQL Server Databases

Wilson Hayes

Copyright © 2025 by Wilson Hayes

All rights reserved.

No part of this book may be reproduced, distributed, or transmitted in any form or by any means, including photocopying, recording, or other electronic or mechanical methods, without the prior written permission of the publisher, except in the case of brief quotations embodied in critical reviews and certain other non-commercial uses permitted by copyright law.

TABLE OF CONTENTS

PART 1: FOUNDATIONS OF SQL SERVER ADMINISTRATION

Chapter 1: Introduction to SQL Server and Database Administration

Understanding the Role of a Database Administrator (DBA)

A **Database Administrator (DBA)** is responsible for the **installation, configuration, maintenance, security, and optimization** of a database system. In organizations where data is the backbone of operations, DBAs play a crucial role in ensuring data **integrity, availability, and performance**.

Why DBAs Are Essential

DBAs are responsible for **keeping data secure, accessible, and efficiently managed**. They ensure that databases are optimized for performance, **troubleshoot issues, implement backups, and protect against data loss**. Without an effective DBA, a business could face **slow performance, security vulnerabilities, data corruption, and even catastrophic data loss**.

Core Responsibilities of a DBA

1. **Database Installation & Configuration** – Setting up and configuring SQL Server based on business needs.

2. **Performance Monitoring & Optimization** – Ensuring queries run efficiently, identifying bottlenecks, and tuning the database.

3. **Security Management** – Controlling access to data, ensuring encryption, and protecting against breaches.

4. **Backup & Recovery** – Implementing backup policies and ensuring recovery procedures in case of failure.

5. **High Availability & Disaster Recovery (HA/DR)** – Configuring systems to ensure minimal downtime and fast recovery.

6. **User & Role Management** – Defining and controlling user access to prevent unauthorized actions.

7. **Automation & Maintenance** – Creating scheduled jobs for backups, updates, and performance monitoring.

8. **Compliance & Auditing** – Ensuring that the database adheres to regulations like GDPR, HIPAA, or SOX.

9. **Scaling & Upgrading** – Managing database growth and ensuring it scales to meet business demands.

10. **Scripting & Automation** – Writing PowerShell scripts or T-SQL commands for automation.

Overview of SQL Server Editions and Features

Microsoft SQL Server is a **relational database management system (RDBMS)** designed for storing, retrieving, and managing structured data efficiently. It supports **transactional processing, business intelligence, and analytics** in organizations of all sizes.

SQL Server Editions

Microsoft offers several SQL Server editions, each catering to different use cases:

1. **Enterprise Edition**

   o Designed for **large-scale applications** with high-performance needs.

- o Features **advanced security, performance tuning, and high availability** tools.

- o Supports **Always On Availability Groups, Transparent Data Encryption (TDE), and Big Data Clusters**.

2. **Standard Edition**

- o Aimed at **medium-sized businesses** that need strong database capabilities without enterprise-level cost.

- o Lacks some high-availability and performance-tuning features found in the **Enterprise Edition**.

3. **Express Edition**

- o A **free, lightweight version** suitable for small applications.

- o Limited in terms of CPU, memory, and storage capacity (e.g., 10GB max database size).

- o Ideal for **learning, small web apps, and lightweight applications**.

4. **Developer Edition**

- o Offers **all features of Enterprise Edition** but **cannot be used in production**.

- o Ideal for **learning, testing, and development purposes**.

5. **Azure SQL Database**

- o A **fully managed cloud-based SQL Server**.

- o Provides **automatic scaling, high availability, and security** without the need for manual maintenance.

- o Supports **serverless and managed instance options**.

SQL Server Architecture and Core Components

SQL Server is built on a **multi-layered architecture**, allowing it to efficiently manage queries, transactions, and data storage. Understanding its architecture helps DBAs optimize performance and troubleshoot issues effectively.

Key Components of SQL Server

1. **Database Engine**

   - The **core service** responsible for **storing, processing, and securing data**.

   - Manages **queries, transactions, indexing, and locking mechanisms**.

2. **SQL Server Agent**

   - Automates administrative tasks like **backups, job scheduling, and monitoring**.

   - Helps DBAs ensure routine maintenance and optimization.

3. **SQL Server Management Studio (SSMS)**

   - A **GUI tool** for managing databases, writing queries, and monitoring performance.

   - Provides **Object Explorer, Query Editor, and Performance Dashboard**.

4. **Transaction Log (T-Log)**

- Stores **all database modifications** to enable rollback and recovery.

- Essential for **point-in-time recovery and high availability solutions**.

5. **SQL Server Integration Services (SSIS)**

   - A **data integration tool** for **ETL (Extract, Transform, Load) processes**.

   - Used for **migrating data between different sources, transforming data, and automating workflows**.

6. **SQL Server Reporting Services (SSRS)**

   - Generates **interactive and paginated reports** from SQL Server data.

   - Used in **business intelligence applications**.

7. **SQL Server Analysis Services (SSAS)**

   - Supports **OLAP (Online Analytical Processing)** and **data mining**.

   - Allows users to analyze large datasets efficiently.

8. **Buffer Pool**

   - Stores frequently accessed data pages in memory to **reduce disk I/O and improve performance**.

9. **SQL Query Optimizer**

   - Determines the **best execution plan** for queries, ensuring efficient database performance.

10. **TempDB**

- A temporary database used for **sorting, aggregations, and session-based data storage**.

- Resets upon **server restart** to free up resources.

Key Responsibilities and Career Path for SQL Server DBAs

A **career in database administration** offers **stability, high salaries, and opportunities for specialization**. DBAs can work in **finance, healthcare, e-commerce, and cloud computing**, among others.

Career Progression in Database Administration

1. **Entry-Level DBA / Junior DBA**

   o Assists with **basic database maintenance.**

   o Monitors **backups, security, and performance.**

   o Gains experience with **SQL queries, indexing, and stored procedures.**

2. **Mid-Level DBA**

   o Manages **database optimization, high availability, and security.**

   o Works with **index tuning, query optimization, and disaster recovery planning.**

   o Handles **SQL Server clustering and replication.**

3. **Senior DBA**

   o Leads **database architecture design, performance tuning, and cloud migrations.**

   o Oversees **database security policies and regulatory compliance.**

- Works on **advanced troubleshooting and capacity planning**.

4. **Database Architect**

   - Designs **scalable and high-availability database systems**.

   - Defines **data governance policies** and **strategic database planning**.

   - Works with **data warehousing, BI solutions, and AI-driven performance tuning**.

5. **Cloud Database Engineer / SQL Consultant**

   - Specializes in **SQL Server on Azure, AWS, or hybrid cloud**.

   - Helps businesses **migrate databases, optimize performance, and implement security best practices**.

   - Works as a **freelance consultant or in enterprise cloud projects**.

Certifications to Boost a DBA Career

1. **Microsoft Certified: Azure Database Administrator Associate (DP-300)** – For cloud-based database management.

2. **Microsoft Certified: Database Administrator (MCDBA)** – Helps establish expertise in SQL Server administration.

3. **Microsoft Certified Solutions Expert (MCSE): Data Management and Analytics** – Focuses on business intelligence and data analytics.

Chapter 2: SQL Server Installation and Configuration Best Practices

SQL Server is one of the most powerful and widely used database management systems, trusted by enterprises to handle vast amounts of data efficiently. However, its performance and stability largely depend on how well it is installed and configured. A poorly planned installation can lead to security vulnerabilities, performance bottlenecks, and system failures.

In this chapter, we will cover the **best practices for SQL Server installation and configuration** to ensure optimal performance, security, and reliability. This includes understanding **system requirements, pre-installation considerations, step-by-step installation, post-installation optimization, and an in-depth look at SQL Server services and components.**

By the end of this chapter, you will have a **clear roadmap** for successfully installing and configuring SQL Server in a production environment.

1. System Requirements and Pre-Installation Considerations

Before installing SQL Server, it is crucial to assess whether your hardware and software environment meets the necessary requirements. A failure to do so can lead to **performance issues, system crashes, or security vulnerabilities**.

1.1. Hardware Requirements

Microsoft SQL Server has specific **hardware requirements** that must be met for a smooth installation. These include:

Processor Requirements

- **Minimum:** 1.4 GHz 64-bit processor

- **Recommended:** 2 GHz or faster, multi-core processor

- **Best Practice:** Use **Intel Xeon or AMD EPYC processors** for enterprise-level performance

Memory (RAM) Requirements

- **Minimum:** 2 GB

- **Recommended:** 8 GB or more

- **Best Practice:** Allocate at least **16 GB for production environments**

Storage Requirements

- **Minimum:** 6 GB of free disk space

- **Recommended:** SSD (Solid-State Drive) for optimal performance

- **Best Practice:** Use RAID 10 for **fault tolerance and high-speed access**

1.2. Software Requirements

SQL Server supports various **Windows operating systems**.

- **Supported OS:**
  - Windows Server 2019, Windows Server 2022
  - Windows 10, Windows 11 (for development/testing only)

- **Required Dependencies:**
  - .NET Framework 4.8 or later
  - Windows PowerShell 5.1 or later

- **SQL Server Edition Selection:**

    o **SQL Server Express:** Free version for lightweight applications

    o **SQL Server Standard:** For mid-sized businesses

    o **SQL Server Enterprise:** For large-scale, high-performance databases

1.3. Pre-Installation Considerations

Before proceeding with the installation, consider the following:

✅ **Account Permissions:** Ensure the installation account has **Administrator rights**.

✅ **Disk Space Planning:** Allocate separate drives for **database files, logs, and backups**.

✅ **Networking Requirements:** Open required ports (default **TCP 1433** for SQL Server).

✅ **Security Hardening:** Disable unnecessary services to **reduce attack surfaces**.

✅ **Backup Plan:** Take a **full system backup** before installation in case of rollbacks.

2. Step-by-Step Installation Guide for SQL Server

2.1. Downloading and Preparing for Installation

1. **Download the SQL Server Installer** from the official Microsoft website.

2. **Verify the Integrity** of the downloaded file using SHA256 checksum.

3. **Disable Antivirus Software Temporarily** to avoid installation conflicts.

2.2. Running the SQL Server Installation Wizard

1. **Launch SQL Server Setup** (setup.exe).

2. **Select "New SQL Server Standalone Installation".**

3. **Accept License Terms** and proceed.

Feature Selection

Choose the components needed:

✅ **Database Engine Services** (Core SQL Server functionality)

✅ **SQL Server Replication** (If using database mirroring or Always On)

✅ **Full-Text Search** (For text-based queries)

✅ **Machine Learning Services** (If using AI/ML within SQL Server)

2.3. Configuring Server and Authentication Modes

Server Configuration

- Choose **"Mixed Mode Authentication"** to support both Windows and SQL Server authentication.

- Set a strong **SA (System Administrator) password** for security.

Instance Configuration

- Default Instance: Named MSSQLSERVER (easier for default settings).

- Named Instance: Useful if **running multiple SQL Server instances** on the same machine.

2.4. Completing the Installation

Once all configurations are set:

- Click **"Install"** and wait for the installation to complete.

- Restart the server if prompted.

- Verify installation using **SQL Server Management Studio (SSMS)**.

3. Post-Installation Configuration for Optimal Performance

After installing SQL Server, it is essential to fine-tune settings for better **performance, security, and stability**.

3.1. Configuring Memory Allocation

- **Limit SQL Server memory usage** to prevent it from consuming all system resources.

- Navigate to **SQL Server Properties > Memory** and set a max limit (e.g., **80% of total RAM**).

3.2. Optimizing TempDB Configuration

TempDB is a **critical system database** that can affect performance. Best practices:

- Use **multiple TempDB files** (one file per CPU core, up to 8).

- Store TempDB on a **separate, fast SSD drive**.

3.3. Enabling SQL Server Performance Monitoring

Use tools like:

- **Dynamic Management Views (DMVs)** to track queries.

- **SQL Profiler and Extended Events** to monitor slow queries.

- **Performance Monitor (PerfMon)** to analyze CPU, memory, and disk usage.

4. Understanding SQL Server Services and Components

SQL Server consists of multiple **services** that perform different roles.

4.1. Core SQL Server Services

Service	Description
SQL Server Database Engine	Handles query processing, transactions, and database storage.

SQL Server Agent	Automates jobs such as backups and index maintenance.
SQL Server Browser	Manages incoming SQL Server connection requests.
SQL Server Reporting Services (SSRS)	Generates business intelligence reports.

4.2. SQL Server Management Tools

Tool	Purpose
SQL Server Management Studio (SSMS)	Graphical interface for database administration.
SQLCMD	Command-line tool for executing SQL scripts.
Azure Data Studio	Modern cross-platform tool for SQL development.

Chapter 3: SQL Server Management Tools and Interfaces

Managing SQL Server effectively requires robust tools that enable database administrators (DBAs) to execute queries, optimize performance, automate tasks, and monitor database health. Microsoft provides a suite of tools to interact with SQL Server, ranging from **graphical user interfaces (GUIs) like SQL Server Management Studio (SSMS)** to **command-line tools like SQLCMD and PowerShell**. Additionally, monitoring and troubleshooting tools such as **SQL Profiler, Extended Events, and Database Mail** help DBAs **track, log, and automate database tasks efficiently**.

This chapter provides a **comprehensive overview** of SQL Server management tools and interfaces, detailing their **features, usage, best practices, and real-world applications**. By the end of this chapter, you will have a deep understanding of the tools available and how to use them effectively for SQL Server administration.

1. SQL Server Management Studio (SSMS) – Features and Usage

1.1. What is SQL Server Management Studio (SSMS)?

SQL Server Management Studio (SSMS) is the primary **GUI-based tool** for managing SQL Server databases. It provides an **intuitive interface** for executing queries, configuring databases, managing security settings, and performing administrative tasks.

Key Features of SSMS:

✅ **Query Execution** – Write and execute SQL queries with an interactive editor.

✅ **Database Management** – Create, modify, and delete databases, tables, and indexes.

✅ **Performance Monitoring** – Analyze query execution plans and optimize performance.

✅ **Security Configuration** – Manage logins, roles, and permissions.

✓ **Backup and Restore** – Perform database backups and recovery operations.

1.2. Installing and Connecting to SQL Server using SSMS

Step 1: Download and Install SSMS

1. Visit the official **Microsoft SQL Server Management Studio** download page.

2. Download the latest **SSMS installer**.

3. Run the installer and follow the installation prompts.

Step 2: Connect to SQL Server

1. Open **SQL Server Management Studio (SSMS)**.

2. In the **Connect to Server** dialog box:

   o Server Type: **Database Engine**

   o Server Name: Enter the SQL Server instance name (e.g., localhost for local installations).

   o Authentication: Choose **Windows Authentication** or **SQL Server Authentication**.

3. Click **Connect** to access the database server.

1.3. Navigating SSMS: Key Tools and Features

Feature	Description
Object Explorer	Provides a hierarchical view of all databases, tables, views, and security settings.
Query Editor	Allows users to write and execute SQL queries. Supports syntax highlighting and execution plans.
Activity Monitor	Displays real-time database performance metrics such as CPU usage, active queries, and wait times.
SQL Server Agent	Automates database jobs such as backups, maintenance, and alerting.

2. Using SQLCMD, Azure Data Studio, and Other Tools

2.1. SQLCMD – The Command-Line Interface for SQL Server

SQLCMD is a command-line utility for executing T-SQL queries, managing databases, and automating administrative tasks.

Advantages of Using SQLCMD:

✅ Lightweight and does not require a GUI.

✅ Ideal for automation through scripts.

✅ Supports remote database connections.

Basic SQLCMD Syntax:

- **Connect to SQL Server:**

sh

```
sqlcmd -S ServerName -U Username -P Password
```

- **Execute a Query:**

sql

```
sqlcmd -S ServerName -Q "SELECT name FROM sys.databases"
```

- **Run a SQL Script:**

sh

```
sqlcmd -S ServerName -i script.sql
```

2.2. Azure Data Studio – A Modern SQL Management Tool

Azure Data Studio is a **cross-platform database tool** for SQL Server and cloud-based databases. Unlike SSMS, which is Windows-only, Azure Data Studio runs on **Windows, Linux, and macOS**.

Why Use Azure Data Studio?

✅ **Lightweight** – Faster than SSMS, with lower memory consumption.

✓ **Built-in Notebooks** – Allows documentation and query execution in the same interface.

✓ **Cloud Integration** – Works seamlessly with **Azure SQL Database**.

3. PowerShell for SQL Server Administration

3.1. Introduction to PowerShell for SQL Server

PowerShell is a powerful scripting language that allows DBAs to automate SQL Server management tasks. The **SQL Server PowerShell module (SqlServer)** extends PowerShell's capabilities for database operations.

Benefits of Using PowerShell for SQL Server:

✓ Automates repetitive DBA tasks.

✓ Reduces human errors in database management.

✓ Enables remote database administration.

3.2. Essential PowerShell Commands for SQL Server

1. List All SQL Server Instances:

powershell

```
Get-Service | Where-Object {$_.DisplayName -like "*SQL*"}
```

2. Execute a SQL Query from PowerShell:

powershell

```
Invoke-Sqlcmd -ServerInstance "ServerName" -Database "master" -Query "SELECT name FROM sys.databases"
```

3. Backup a Database Using PowerShell:

powershell

```
Backup-SqlDatabase -ServerInstance "ServerName" -Database "MyDatabase" -BackupFile "C:\Backups\MyDatabase.bak"
```

4. Database Mail, SQL Profiler, and Extended Events

4.1. Configuring Database Mail for Automated Notifications

Database Mail allows SQL Server to send email notifications for alerts and job executions.

Step 1: Enable Database Mail

sql

EXEC sp_configure 'Database Mail XPs', 1;

RECONFIGURE;

Step 2: Configure a Mail Profile

1. Open **SSMS** and go to **Database Mail Configuration Wizard**.

2. Create a new **Mail Profile** and configure SMTP settings.

3. Assign users to the mail profile.

Step 3: Send a Test Email

sql

```
EXEC msdb.dbo.sp_send_dbmail

  @profile_name = 'MyProfile',

  @recipients = 'admin@example.com',

  @subject = 'Test Email',

  @body = 'SQL Server Database Mail is working!';
```

4.2. SQL Server Profiler – Real-Time Query Monitoring

SQL Server Profiler is a GUI tool used for **monitoring and troubleshooting database performance**.

How to Use SQL Server Profiler:

1. Open **SQL Server Profiler** from SSMS.

2. Click **"New Trace"** and connect to a database.

3. Select events such as **SQL:BatchCompleted** to monitor executed queries.

4. Click **"Run"** to start tracing SQL activity.

4.3. Extended Events – The Modern Alternative to SQL Profiler

Extended Events (XEvents) is a **lightweight event-tracing tool** that replaces SQL Profiler in modern SQL Server versions.

Steps to Create an Extended Event Session in SSMS:

1. In SSMS, navigate to **Management > Extended Events > Sessions**.

2. Right-click and select **"New Session Wizard"**.

3. Select events like **query performance, deadlocks, and wait times**.

4. Configure a target (e.g., event file for analysis).

5. Start the session to capture real-time database events.

PART 2: DATABASE DESIGN, STORAGE, AND PERFORMANCE OPTIMIZATION

Chapter 4: Database Design and Architecture for High Performance

A well-designed database architecture is fundamental to ensuring **high performance, scalability, and efficiency** in SQL Server environments. Poor database design can lead to **slow queries, inefficient storage, and excessive resource consumption**, which impact overall system performance.

This chapter explores the **best practices for database design** by covering key concepts such as **normalization, indexing, partitioning, choosing appropriate data types, OLTP vs. OLAP table design, and schema management**. By the end of this chapter, you will be equipped with the knowledge to build optimized and scalable databases that support mission-critical applications.

1. Understanding Normalization, Indexing, and Partitioning

1.1. Database Normalization: Structuring Data for Efficiency

Normalization is the process of organizing database tables to **reduce redundancy and improve data integrity**. It helps minimize **data anomalies** and ensures **efficient query performance**.

Normalization Forms and Their Use Cases

Normalization Level	Description	Use Case
1NF (First Normal Form)	Eliminates duplicate columns and ensures atomic values.	Basic data consistency.
2NF (Second Normal Form)	Ensures that all non-key attributes are functionally dependent on the primary key.	Avoids partial dependencies.

3NF (Third Normal Form)	Removes transitive dependencies (non-key attributes should not depend on other non-key attributes).	Reduces redundant data storage.
BCNF (Boyce-Codd Normal Form)	A stricter version of 3NF, ensuring no overlapping candidate keys.	Enforces strong data integrity.

Example of Normalization:

Unnormalized Table:

OrderID	CustomerName	Product	Price
101	John Doe	Laptop	1200
101	John Doe	Mouse	25

Normalized Structure (1NF & 2NF applied):

- **Orders Table:**

OrderID	CustomerID	OrderDate
101	1	2024-03-10

- **Customers Table:**

CustomerID	CustomerName
1	John Doe

- **OrderDetails Table:**

OrderID	ProductID	Price
101	1	1200
101	2	25

Normalization Benefits:

✓ Reduces redundant data storage.

✓ Enhances data integrity.

✓ Improves query consistency.

1.2. Indexing: Improving Query Performance

Indexes **accelerate query performance** by allowing SQL Server to **quickly locate data** without scanning entire tables.

Types of Indexes and Their Use Cases

Index Type	Description	Use Case
Clustered Index	Sorts and stores the data rows in the table based on the key column.	Used for **primary keys**.
Non-Clustered Index	Stores index separately from table data, improving lookup speed.	Used for **frequently searched columns**.
Full-Text Index	Optimized for text-based searches.	Used in **search engines**.
Filtered Index	Indexes only specific rows of a table.	Useful for **large datasets** with selective queries.

Best Practices for Indexing:

✅ Avoid **over-indexing**, which can slow down INSERT and UPDATE operations.

✅ Use **covering indexes** to include all necessary columns for query execution.

✅ Regularly **rebuild and reorganize indexes** to maintain efficiency.

Example of Creating a Non-Clustered Index:

sql

```
CREATE NONCLUSTERED INDEX idx_CustomerName
ON Customers (CustomerName);
```

1.3. Partitioning: Managing Large Datasets Efficiently

Partitioning helps manage **large datasets** by splitting tables and indexes into smaller, more manageable pieces.

Benefits of Partitioning:

✅ Enhances **query performance** for large datasets.

✅ Improves **backup and maintenance efficiency**.

✅ Enables **data archiving strategies**.

Example: Creating a Partitioned Table by Year

sql

```
CREATE PARTITION FUNCTION RangePartition (INT)

AS RANGE LEFT FOR VALUES (2019, 2020, 2021, 2022);
```

2. Choosing the Right Data Types and Storage Structures

2.1. Impact of Data Types on Performance

Choosing the **right data types** ensures **efficient storage utilization** and **query performance**.

Data Type	Use Case	Storage Impact
INT	Whole numbers (IDs, counters)	4 bytes
BIGINT	Large numbers (billions)	8 bytes
VARCHAR(N)	Variable-length text	Uses only needed space

NVARCHAR(N)	Unicode text (multilingual support)	Takes more storage
DATETIME	Timestamps	8 bytes

Best Practices:

✓ Use **appropriate data types** to minimize storage space.

✓ Prefer **VARCHAR** over **CHAR** for variable-length text fields.

✓ Use **DATE instead of DATETIME** if time is not needed.

3. Table Design Best Practices for OLTP and OLAP Workloads

3.1. OLTP vs. OLAP Table Design

Feature	OLTP (Online Transaction Processing)	OLAP (Online Analytical Processing)
Focus	Transactional data (insert/update-heavy)	Analytical queries (read-heavy)

Normalization	Highly normalized for integrity	Denormalized for speed
Indexes	Fewer indexes for write efficiency	More indexes for fast reads
Partitioning	Not always needed	Often partitioned for performance

3.2. Best Practices for Table Design

✔ Use **Primary Keys and Foreign Keys** for integrity.

✔ Optimize **indexing strategies** based on workload (OLTP vs. OLAP).

✔ Avoid using **NULLable columns** unless necessary.

✔ Implement **row compression** for large datasets.

4. Schema and Object Management

4.1. Organizing Database Schemas

A well-structured schema improves **security, maintainability, and performance**.

Best Practices for Schema Design

✅ Group objects into **schemas** to improve security (e.g., Sales.Orders vs. HR.Employees).

✅ Use **meaningful names** for tables, views, and indexes.

✅ Regularly **clean up unused objects** to avoid clutter.

Example: Creating a Schema for HR Data

sql

```sql
CREATE SCHEMA HR;
GO
CREATE TABLE HR.Employees (
    EmployeeID INT PRIMARY KEY,
    FullName VARCHAR(100),
    Salary DECIMAL(10,2)
);
```

Chapter 5: Indexing and Query Performance Optimization

In SQL Server, **indexing and query optimization** are critical for maintaining database performance, ensuring that queries execute efficiently without excessive resource consumption. A well-designed indexing strategy can significantly reduce **CPU usage, memory consumption, and I/O operations**, leading to **faster data retrieval and improved overall system responsiveness**.

This chapter explores **the fundamentals of indexing, query execution plans, and performance tuning strategies** to help database administrators (DBAs) and developers optimize SQL Server for high-performance workloads. We will cover:

- **Clustered vs. Non-Clustered Indexes**

- **Index Maintenance and Performance Tuning Strategies**

- **Understanding Query Execution Plans**

- **Using Query Store and Dynamic Management Views (DMVs)**

By the end of this chapter, you will have a **comprehensive understanding** of how to design, manage, and optimize indexes to enhance SQL Server performance.

1. Clustered vs. Non-Clustered Indexes

Indexes in SQL Server are **data structures that improve query performance** by allowing faster retrieval of rows. Without indexes, SQL Server performs **full table scans**, which are slow and resource-intensive.

1.1. What is a Clustered Index?

A **clustered index** determines the **physical order of data storage** in a table. Since the table data is **physically sorted** based on the clustered index key, only **one clustered index** can exist per table.

Key Characteristics of Clustered Indexes:

✅ **Physically sorts data** in storage.

✅ **Automatically created** on the primary key unless specified otherwise.

✅ **Efficient for range-based queries and sequential data retrieval.**

Example: Creating a Clustered Index on a Primary Key

sql

```sql
CREATE CLUSTERED INDEX IX_Customers_ID
ON Customers (CustomerID);
```

1.2. What is a Non-Clustered Index?

A **non-clustered index** stores pointers to data rather than physically sorting it. It speeds up lookups for frequently queried columns but requires additional storage.

Key Characteristics of Non-Clustered Indexes:

✅ **Does not change the physical order** of data in a table.

✅ **Supports multiple indexes** per table.

✅ **Best for filtering specific column values.**

Example: Creating a Non-Clustered Index for Searching by Email

sql

```sql
CREATE NONCLUSTERED INDEX IX_Customers_Email
ON Customers (Email);
```

1.3. Clustered vs. Non-Clustered Index Performance Comparison

Feature	Clustered Index	Non-Clustered Index
Storage	Physically orders data	Stores pointers to rows
Speed	Faster for range scans and sorting	Faster for specific lookups
Best For	Primary keys, sequential queries	Search-heavy queries, multiple lookups
Number Per Table	One per table	Multiple per table

2. Index Maintenance and Performance Tuning Strategies

Indexes improve performance, but they **require regular maintenance** to prevent fragmentation and inefficiencies.

2.1. Identifying Fragmented Indexes

Fragmentation occurs when **index pages are scattered**, leading to inefficient queries. SQL Server provides **Dynamic Management Views (DMVs)** to identify fragmented indexes.

Check Index Fragmentation:

sql

```sql
SELECT dbschemas.[name] AS 'Schema',

    dbtables.[name] AS 'Table',

    dbindexes.[name] AS 'Index',

    indexstats.avg_fragmentation_in_percent

FROM   sys.dm_db_index_physical_stats(DB_ID(),   NULL,
NULL, NULL, 'LIMITED') AS indexstats

JOIN   sys.tables   dbtables   ON   dbtables.[object_id]   =
indexstats.[object_id]

JOIN   sys.schemas   dbschemas   ON   dbtables.[schema_id]   =
dbschemas.[schema_id]

JOIN   sys.indexes   dbindexes   ON   dbindexes.[object_id]   =
dbtables.[object_id]
```

WHERE indexstats.avg_fragmentation_in_percent > 10;

2.2. Rebuilding vs. Reorganizing Indexes

Operation	When to Use	Command
Reorganize	When fragmentation is **10–30%**	ALTER INDEX ALL ON TableName REORGANIZE;
Rebuild	When fragmentation is **above 30%**	ALTER INDEX ALL ON TableName REBUILD;

2.3. Removing Unused Indexes

Unused indexes **consume storage** and **slow down INSERT/UPDATE operations**. Identify and drop unused indexes using the following query:

sql

SELECT name, index_id, user_seeks, user_scans, user_lookups, user_updates

FROM sys.dm_db_index_usage_stats

WHERE database_id = DB_ID() AND user_seeks = 0 AND user_scans = 0;

Drop an Unused Index:

sql

DROP INDEX IX_Customers_Email ON Customers;

3. Understanding Query Execution Plans

3.1. What is a Query Execution Plan?

A **query execution plan** is an **optimizer-generated roadmap** that SQL Server follows to execute queries efficiently.

Types of Execution Plans:

✅ **Estimated Execution Plan** – Predicts query execution before running it.

✅ **Actual Execution Plan** – Shows the exact steps SQL Server took to execute the query.

View the Execution Plan in SSMS:

sql

```sql
SET SHOWPLAN_XML ON;

SELECT * FROM Orders WHERE OrderDate > '2024-01-01';

SET SHOWPLAN_XML OFF;
```

3.2. Interpreting Execution Plan Components

Component	Description
Index Seek	Fastest way to retrieve data using an index.
Index Scan	Reads entire index pages (slower than an Index Seek).
Table Scan	Reads entire table (very slow for large datasets).

Optimizing Queries Based on Execution Plan:
✓ Convert **Table Scans** to **Index Seeks** by creating appropriate indexes.

✓ Reduce **high-cost operations** like **Sort and Hash Joins**.

✅ Rewrite queries using **JOINs instead of subqueries**.

4. Using Query Store and Dynamic Management Views (DMVs)

4.1. Query Store: Tracking and Analyzing Query Performance

Query Store captures query history, execution plans, and performance trends.

Enable Query Store:

sql

```
ALTER DATABASE AdventureWorks2019 SET QUERY_STORE = ON;
```

View Top Resource-Consuming Queries:

sql

```
SELECT top 10 query_id, total_execution_count, total_elapsed_time

FROM sys.query_store_runtime_stats

ORDER BY total_elapsed_time DESC;
```

4.2. Dynamic Management Views (DMVs) for Query Performance Analysis

SQL Server **DMVs** provide real-time insights into database performance.

Find Top 5 Slowest Queries:

sql

```
SELECT TOP 5 total_worker_time, execution_count, text

FROM sys.dm_exec_query_stats

CROSS APPLY sys.dm_exec_sql_text(sql_handle)

ORDER BY total_worker_time DESC;
```

Chapter 6: SQL Server Storage, Backup, and Recovery Strategies

In a SQL Server environment, the importance of **storage management, backup strategies, and recovery techniques** cannot be overstated. Proper configuration of **filegroups, data files, and log files** is essential for both performance and recoverability. Similarly, the development of **robust backup strategies** ensures that the database is protected from data loss, while **recovery models** define how SQL Server will recover from failures.

This chapter provides in-depth coverage of SQL Server's **storage architecture, backup strategies, and recovery options**. We will explore the essentials of managing **filegroups, implementing optimal storage configurations**, and the three major types of **backups: full, differential, and transaction log backups**. Additionally, we will cover **SQL Server recovery models** and how to implement **point-in-time recovery**.

By the end of this chapter, you will be well-equipped with the tools and knowledge necessary to implement **robust, efficient, and reliable backup and recovery strategies** for your SQL Server databases.

1. SQL Server Filegroups, Data Files, and Log Files

1.1. SQL Server Filegroups: Organization and Usage

In SQL Server, **filegroups** are used to **group database files** for efficient data storage management and optimized performance. A **filegroup** contains one or more **data files** that store the actual database data.

Types of Filegroups

- **Primary Filegroup**: Contains the system and user-defined tables by default. It is where the primary data file (.mdf) is located.

- **Secondary Filegroups**: Created for organizing data across multiple filegroups. These are optional and can be used for placing non-system tables, indexes, and large objects in separate filegroups.

- **Read-Only Filegroup**: This filegroup allows data to be **only read**. It is useful for archiving purposes or for storing historical data that is rarely modified.

- **Filegroup for Indexes**: You can also create a separate filegroup for **index storage** to improve the performance of large tables by spreading the I/O load across multiple disks.

Best Practices for Filegroups

- Use **multiple filegroups** to distribute large tables or indexes, especially for large-scale systems.

- Place **non-clustered indexes** on separate filegroups to optimize I/O performance during queries.

- **Avoid putting all data** in the primary filegroup as it may result in inefficient disk usage and slowdowns.

Example: Creating a New Filegroup

sql

```
ALTER DATABASE MyDatabase

ADD FILEGROUP SecondaryFG;

GO

ALTER DATABASE MyDatabase
```

```
ADD   FILE   (NAME   =   'DataFile2',   FILENAME   =
'C:\SQLData\MyDatabase_Data2.ndf')   TO   FILEGROUP
SecondaryFG;

GO
```

1.2. SQL Server Data Files

SQL Server uses **data files** (.mdf and .ndf) to store the actual data. These files contain the information of user-defined objects, tables, and indexes.

Types of Data Files

- **Primary Data File (.mdf)**: Every SQL Server database has one primary data file, which holds the database schema and data.

- **Secondary Data File (.ndf)**: These are optional files used for extending the database storage. They are used when a database grows beyond the size that can be handled by the primary file.

Best Practices for Data Files

- **Place data files** across multiple physical disks to balance the **I/O load**.

- Ensure that **each data file** is located on a separate **disk subsystem** to enhance performance.

1.3. SQL Server Log Files

SQL Server uses **log files** (.ldf) to store **transaction logs** that record all the changes made to the database. The **transaction log** ensures that SQL Server can recover the database after a crash.

Log File Characteristics

- **Transaction Logging**: The log file stores every **INSERT, UPDATE, DELETE**, and database schema modification.

- **Recycling of Logs**: SQL Server will recycle log space once the transaction log is backed up (in the case of the **full** or **differential backup**).

Best Practices for Log Files

- Keep log files on a **separate physical drive** from data files to improve performance.

- Ensure that **log files are large enough** to handle the database's daily transactional load to avoid frequent auto-growth events.

- Use **transaction log backups** to prevent the log from growing indefinitely and to ensure you can recover the database to a specific point in time.

Example: Adding a Log File

sql

```
ALTER DATABASE MyDatabase

ADD LOG FILE (NAME = 'LogFile2', FILENAME = 'D:\SQLLogs\MyDatabase_Log2.ldf');

GO
```

2. Best Practices for Storage Optimization

2.1. Choosing Storage Devices for SQL Server

The performance of your SQL Server environment is highly dependent on the **storage devices** used. SQL Server databases are **I/O-intensive** and benefit greatly from optimized disk subsystems.

Best Storage Options

- **Solid-State Drives (SSDs)**: SSDs provide **much faster data access speeds** than traditional Hard Disk Drives (HDDs) and should be used for transaction logs and frequently accessed data.

- **RAID Configurations**: RAID 10 is generally recommended for SQL Server as it provides both **mirrored** and **striped** data, which improves both **performance** and **fault tolerance**.

- **SAN/NAS Storage**: For larger environments or highly available systems, a **Storage Area Network (SAN)** or **Network Attached Storage (NAS)** can be used.

2.2. Storage Best Practices for SQL Server

- **Use Multiple Disks**: Spread the **data files** and **log files** across multiple physical disks to reduce I/O contention.

- **Allocate Adequate Disk Space**: Monitor **disk usage** to ensure that there is always enough space for growth, especially for transaction logs.

- **Optimize Auto-growth Settings**: Set **auto-growth** to a reasonable value to avoid frequent growth operations, which can lead to fragmentation.

3. Backup Strategies: Full, Differential, and Transaction Log Backups

3.1. Understanding Backup Types

SQL Server provides several **backup types** that can be used individually or in combination to create an effective backup strategy.

Full Backup

A **full backup** includes all the data in the database, making it the most complete form of backup. It is typically the **starting point** for any recovery strategy.

Example: Creating a Full Backup

sql

```
BACKUP DATABASE MyDatabase

TO DISK = 'D:\Backups\MyDatabase_Full.bak';

GO
```

Differential Backup

A **differential backup** includes all the changes made since the last **full backup**. This allows for faster restores by reducing the amount of data needed to be backed up.

Example: Creating a Differential Backup

sql

```
BACKUP DATABASE MyDatabase

TO DISK = 'D:\Backups\MyDatabase_Diff.bak'

WITH DIFFERENTIAL;

GO
```

Transaction Log Backup

A **transaction log backup** backs up the transaction log and is essential for **point-in-time recovery**. It allows you to capture all transactions that occurred since the last log backup.

Example: Creating a Transaction Log Backup

sql

BACKUP LOG MyDatabase

TO DISK = 'D:\Backups\MyDatabase_Log.trn';

GO

3.2. Creating an Effective Backup Strategy

An effective backup strategy ensures **data consistency, quick recovery times**, and **minimal downtime**.

Recommended Backup Strategy

1. **Full Backups**: Perform a **weekly full backup**.

2. **Differential Backups**: Take **daily differential backups** to capture changes.

3. **Transaction Log Backups**: Perform **transaction log backups every 15 minutes** (for high-volume databases).

4. Database Recovery Models and Point-in-Time Recovery

4.1. SQL Server Recovery Models

SQL Server provides three main **recovery models** that determine the types of backups you can take and how you can recover data.

Full Recovery Model

The **Full Recovery Model** allows for **complete point-in-time recovery**. It records all transactions, enabling you to restore the database to the **exact point in time** before a failure.

Best Practices

- Ideal for databases with **high transaction volumes**.

- Requires frequent **transaction log backups** to prevent the log file from growing too large.

Simple Recovery Model

The **Simple Recovery Model** only supports **full and differential backups**. It does not keep the transaction log beyond the last checkpoint, making point-in-time recovery impossible.

Best Practices

- Suitable for **low transaction databases** where point-in-time recovery is not required.

- Use for databases where performance is a higher priority than recoverability.

Bulk-Logged Recovery Model

The **Bulk-Logged Recovery Model** is similar to the **Full Recovery Model**, but it **minimizes logging overhead** for bulk operations (e.g., **bulk imports**). However, it still supports **point-in-time recovery** for most cases.

Best Practices

- Ideal for **databases that handle large bulk operations**.

4.2. Implementing Point-in-Time Recovery

Point-in-time recovery allows you to restore a database to a **specific moment** in time, useful in cases where data corruption or accidental data modification occurs.

Steps for Point-in-Time Recovery:

1. **Restore the Full Backup**:

sql

```sql
RESTORE DATABASE MyDatabase

FROM DISK = 'D:\Backups\MyDatabase_Full.bak';

GO
```

2. **Restore the Differential Backup (if applicable)**:

sql

```sql
RESTORE DATABASE MyDatabase

FROM DISK = 'D:\Backups\MyDatabase_Diff.bak'

WITH NORECOVERY;

GO
```

3. **Restore Transaction Logs**:

sql

```sql
RESTORE LOG MyDatabase

FROM DISK = 'D:\Backups\MyDatabase_Log.trn'

WITH STOPAT = '2024-03-10T12:00:00';

GO
```

PART 3: SECURITY, HIGH AVAILABILITY, AND DISASTER RECOVERY

Chapter 7: SQL Server Security and Access Control

SQL Server is one of the most widely used relational database management systems (RDBMS) in the world, making its security an absolute priority. With SQL Server storing vast amounts of sensitive and business-critical data, ensuring its **confidentiality, integrity, and availability** is paramount. Effective **access control** and **authentication** strategies help ensure that only authorized users can access the system and its data. In addition to basic user access control, SQL Server provides a suite of features like **Transparent Data Encryption (TDE)** and **Always Encrypted** to further enhance the security of your database.

This chapter will cover the following essential areas of **SQL Server Security**:

- **Authentication and Authorization Models**

- **Configuring Logins, Users, and Roles**

- **Transparent Data Encryption (TDE)** and **Always Encrypted**

- **Security Auditing and Compliance Best Practices**

By the end of this chapter, you will have a solid understanding of the tools and techniques for implementing **SQL Server security** and ensuring that your database remains secure from unauthorized access or potential threats.

1. Authentication and Authorization Models

1.1. Understanding Authentication Models

SQL Server supports **two types of authentication**: **Windows Authentication** and **SQL Server Authentication**. Both models offer different methods for **verifying the identity of users**.

1.1.1. Windows Authentication

This model integrates with the **Windows operating system** to authenticate users. It uses **Active Directory (AD)** to validate users, allowing them to connect to SQL Server using their Windows credentials.

- **How It Works**: When a user attempts to connect to SQL Server, the system checks their **Windows credentials** (username and password) against Active Directory. If the credentials are valid, the user is authenticated and granted access.

- **Best Practice**: **Windows Authentication** is preferred for SQL Server security because it integrates with Active Directory, is **easier to manage**, and benefits from the advanced security mechanisms that Windows provides, including **Kerberos authentication**, **password policies**, and **account lockout policies**.

1.1.2. SQL Server Authentication

This model relies on SQL Server to authenticate users based on SQL Server-specific credentials (a username and password stored within the database).

- **How It Works**: Users must supply both a **username** and **password** that are defined within the SQL Server instance. SQL Server authenticates these credentials without needing to interact with Windows authentication.

- **Best Practice**: SQL Server Authentication should be **used sparingly**, mainly in situations where **Windows Authentication** is not available or feasible (e.g., connecting from non-Windows operating systems).

1.1.3. Mixed Mode Authentication

In **Mixed Mode Authentication**, SQL Server allows both **Windows Authentication** and **SQL Server Authentication**. This option can be configured during SQL Server installation and is often used in environments where both types of authentication are needed.

- **Best Practice**: **Use Mixed Mode Authentication** only when absolutely necessary, as it increases the potential attack surface. If possible, prefer **Windows Authentication** for tighter security.

1.2. Authorization Models: Managing Permissions

Once a user is authenticated, SQL Server needs to determine what level of access that user should have. This is where **authorization** comes in. SQL Server provides a role-based authorization model using **logins**, **users**, and **roles**.

1.2.1. Logins

A **login** is the object used to authenticate a user to SQL Server. It defines the **identity** of a user or group and is associated with a particular SQL Server instance.

- **How Logins Work**: A login provides access to the **SQL Server instance** and must be mapped to a **user** in each database that the login requires access to.

- **Types of Logins**:

- o **Windows Logins**: For users authenticated via Windows.

- o **SQL Server Logins**: For users authenticated by SQL Server.

- o **Contained Logins**: A feature where logins are created within a specific database and are not tied to the SQL Server instance.

1.2.2. Users and Roles

- **Users**: A **user** in SQL Server is associated with a specific **database**. A user is created for each login that needs access to the database, and this user is granted permissions to perform specific actions within that database.

- **Roles**: **Roles** are collections of permissions that can be assigned to users or groups. SQL Server provides both **fixed database roles** (such as **db_owner, db_datareader, db_datawriter**) and the ability to create **custom roles** with specific permissions tailored to organizational needs.

1.2.3. Granting Permissions

SQL Server supports various **permissions** that can be granted at the **database** or **object level**. Permissions can be granted or denied using **GRANT, DENY,** and **REVOKE** commands. For example:

sql

GRANT SELECT ON dbo.Customers TO UserName;

- **Best Practice**: Use **roles** to simplify security management. Avoid assigning permissions directly to users unless absolutely necessary.

2. Configuring Logins, Users, and Roles

2.1. Creating a Login and User

To grant access to a database, you first need to create a **login** at the **SQL Server instance level** and then map that login to a **user** in the desired database.

Step 1: Create a SQL Server Login

sql

```
CREATE LOGIN NewLogin WITH PASSWORD = 'StrongPassword123';
```

Step 2: Create a Database User

Once the login is created, map it to a user in the database:

sql

```
USE MyDatabase;

CREATE USER NewUser FOR LOGIN NewLogin;
```

Step 3: Assign Roles to the User

Grant appropriate **roles** to the user based on the level of access needed:

sql

```
ALTER ROLE db_datareader ADD MEMBER NewUser;
```

2.2. Best Practices for Role Management

- **Use Fixed Database Roles**: SQL Server provides several built-in roles with predefined permissions. For example, **db_owner** has full control of the database, and **db_datareader** allows read access.

- **Create Custom Roles**: Custom roles can be created if specific permissions are required beyond the built-in roles. This reduces the risk of granting excessive permissions.

- **Principle of Least Privilege**: Always assign the **least amount of privilege** necessary for users to perform their job functions.

3. Transparent Data Encryption (TDE) and Always Encrypted

3.1. Transparent Data Encryption (TDE)

Transparent Data Encryption (TDE) helps protect SQL Server data files by encrypting the **database files (data and log files)** at the storage level. This encryption is transparent, meaning applications do not need to be aware of it. The encryption and decryption occur **automatically** when the data is written to or read from disk.

How TDE Works

- **Encryption Key**: TDE uses a **database encryption key (DEK)**, which is protected by a **server certificate**. The DEK is automatically applied to data and log files as they are written to disk.

- **Use Case**: TDE is useful for protecting data at rest, especially in environments where **compliance regulations** like **PCI-DSS** or **HIPAA** require encryption of sensitive data.

Enabling TDE:

sql

```
CREATE DATABASE MyEncryptedDB;

GO

USE MyEncryptedDB;

GO
```

```
CREATE DATABASE ENCRYPTION KEY;

CREATE CERTIFICATE MyCertificate WITH SUBJECT =
'TDE Certificate';

GO

ALTER DATABASE MyEncryptedDB SET ENCRYPTION
ON;
```

3.2. Always Encrypted

Always Encrypted is a feature that allows SQL Server to **encrypt sensitive data at the column level**. Unlike TDE, which encrypts the entire database, Always Encrypted ensures that sensitive data is **always encrypted in transit and at rest**. The encryption keys are **never exposed to SQL Server**, meaning SQL Server administrators cannot see the plaintext data.

How Always Encrypted Works

- **Column-Level Encryption**: The user can specify which columns in a table should be encrypted. SQL

Server will encrypt/decrypt these columns automatically without revealing the encryption key.

- **Use Case**: Always Encrypted is ideal for **protecting sensitive data** like credit card numbers or personal identification numbers (PINs), especially in **compliance-driven environments**.

Setting Up Always Encrypted:

1. **Create Column Encryption Key**:

sql

```
CREATE COLUMN ENCRYPTION KEY
MyColumnEncryptionKey WITH VALUES
('StrongEncryptionKey123');
```

2. **Encrypt Columns**:

sql

```
CREATE TABLE Customer (
    CustomerID INT,
```

```
CreditCardNumber      NVARCHAR(100)     COLLATE
Latin1_General_BIN        ENCRYPTED        WITH
(COLUMN_ENCRYPTION_KEY                =
MyColumnEncryptionKey,    ENCRYPTION_TYPE    =
Randomized)

);
```

4. Security Auditing and Compliance Best Practices

4.1. Auditing SQL Server Activities

SQL Server provides multiple ways to track and audit database activity. Proper auditing is critical for monitoring security, compliance, and troubleshooting.

Using SQL Server Audit:

SQL Server Audit allows administrators to track and log specific actions, such as **login attempts**, **data modifications**, and **permissions changes**. The audit logs can be directed to **SQL Server logs** or a file.

Creating an Audit Specification:

sql

```
CREATE SERVER AUDIT MyAudit

TO FILE (FILEPATH = 'C:\AuditLogs\');

GO

CREATE SERVER AUDIT SPECIFICATION MyAuditSpec

FOR SERVER AUDIT MyAudit

ADD (FAILED_LOGIN_GROUP);

GO

ALTER SERVER AUDIT MyAudit WITH (STATE = ON);
```

Best Practices:

- **Enable auditing** for sensitive actions like failed login attempts, data changes, and schema modifications.

- Regularly review **audit logs** for suspicious activities.

4.2. Compliance Considerations

SQL Server provides **security features** that help meet compliance requirements for regulations like **HIPAA, PCI-**

DSS, and GDPR. Regularly check for updates to ensure that your SQL Server environment aligns with the latest compliance standards.

Compliance Best Practices:

- **Encryption**: Use TDE and Always Encrypted for data protection.

- **Access Control**: Follow the **least privilege principle**.

- **Audit Trails**: Maintain audit logs and ensure they are regularly reviewed.

- **Patch Management**: Regularly apply security patches provided by Microsoft.

Chapter 8: High Availability and Disaster Recovery (HA/DR) Solutions

In today's world, data is a critical asset for businesses of all sizes. For SQL Server environments, ensuring **high availability (HA)** and **disaster recovery (DR)** is essential to safeguard against system failures, data loss, and prolonged downtime. Having a **comprehensive HA/DR solution** enables organizations to continue operating even in the face of hardware failures, software issues, or natural disasters.

In this chapter, we will delve into SQL Server's **High Availability** and **Disaster Recovery (HA/DR)** solutions. We will explore several strategies to ensure your SQL Server environment is **always available** and that you can **recover data quickly** when an outage occurs. The key solutions discussed will include:

- **SQL Server Always On Availability Groups**

- **Database Mirroring, Log Shipping, and Replication**

- **Failover Clustering and Disaster Recovery Planning**

- **Testing and Automating DR Scenarios**

By the end of this chapter, you will understand how to implement **robust HA/DR strategies** that ensure **data availability** and **business continuity**.

1. SQL Server Always On Availability Groups

1.1. Overview of Always On Availability Groups

Introduced in SQL Server 2012, **Always On Availability Groups** (AGs) offer a highly available and disaster-tolerant solution that allows **multiple copies of a database** (called **availability replicas**) to be synchronized across different servers. With AGs, you can achieve **automatic failover** and **data redundancy** with minimal downtime.

Key Features of Always On AGs:

- **Multiple replicas**: Support for up to **eight replicas** of a database.

- **Automatic failover**: When the primary replica fails, the secondary replica automatically takes over.

- **Readable secondary replicas**: Allow read-only workloads to be offloaded to secondary replicas.

- **Support for different availability modes**: **Synchronous** and **Asynchronous**.

Architecture of Always On AGs:

- **Primary Replica**: The primary replica is the read-write database instance that handles all client connections.

- **Secondary Replicas**: These are the standby instances that store copies of the database. In **synchronous** mode, the data is replicated in real time; in **asynchronous** mode, the replication happens with a lag.

- **Availability Group Listener**: A virtual network name that clients use to connect to the availability group, which points to the current primary replica.

1.2. Configuring Always On Availability Groups

To implement Always On AGs, certain prerequisites must be met, including setting up **Windows Server Failover Clustering** (WSFC) and ensuring that **SQL Server Enterprise Edition** is used. The following steps outline the process of configuring Always On AGs:

Step 1: Enable Always On AGs on SQL Server

1. Open **SQL Server Configuration Manager**.

2. Under **SQL Server Services**, right-click the **SQL Server** instance and select **Properties**.

3. Under the **Always On High Availability** tab, enable **Always On Availability Groups** and restart SQL Server.

Step 2: Set Up Windows Server Failover Cluster

1. Create a **Windows Server Failover Cluster** (WSFC) to manage failover capabilities.

2. Ensure that the cluster nodes are running **Windows Server 2012 or higher**.

3. Use **Cluster Manager** to validate the cluster configuration.

Step 3: Configure the Availability Group

1. Use **SQL Server Management Studio (SSMS)** to create an availability group.

2. Specify the **primary database**, choose the **secondary replicas**, and configure the **failover mode** (synchronous or asynchronous).

3. Set up the **availability group listener**, which will manage client redirection to the primary replica during failovers.

Step 4: Synchronize the Databases

Once the availability group is set up, SQL Server will begin **synchronizing** the database between the primary and secondary replicas. You can use **synchronous-commit mode** for real-time data replication or **asynchronous-commit mode** if a slight data lag is acceptable.

1.3. Managing Always On Availability Groups

Managing Always On AGs involves monitoring replica health, synchronizing databases, and handling failover events. Some key tasks include:

- **Monitoring Replica Health**: Always On Availability Groups can be monitored using **SQL Server Management Studio (SSMS), Dynamic Management Views (DMVs),** and **SQL Server Profiler**.

- **Manual Failover**: In situations where the primary replica needs to be manually failed over (e.g., for maintenance), administrators can initiate a **planned failover** from SSMS.

- **Backup Strategies for AGs**: Always On supports backup operations from either the **primary replica** or **secondary replica** (for read-only workloads). It is recommended to back up the database from the secondary replica to reduce load on the primary replica.

2. Database Mirroring, Log Shipping, and Replication

While Always On Availability Groups are a powerful HA/DR solution, other methods like **database mirroring**, **log shipping**, and **replication** have been used for years and are still viable options depending on your organization's needs.

2.1. Database Mirroring

Database Mirroring is a high-availability solution that maintains two copies of a database: a **primary** and a **mirror**. Mirroring can be configured to work in either **synchronous** or

asynchronous modes. It is important to note that Microsoft is **deprecating database mirroring** in favor of Always On AGs.

Configuration Steps:

1. **Set Up Principal and Mirror Instances**: The principal database is the primary source of data, and the mirror database is an exact copy of the principal.

2. **Configure the Witness Server**: The witness server helps in automatic failover by monitoring the health of the principal server.

3. **Monitor Mirroring**: Use **SQL Server Management Studio** to monitor the status of database mirroring.

2.2. Log Shipping

Log Shipping is a disaster recovery solution where **transaction log backups** from the primary database are automatically copied to a secondary server. These log backups are then applied to the secondary server.

How Log Shipping Works:

1. **Backup**: A transaction log backup is taken from the primary server at regular intervals.

2. **Copy**: The log backup is copied to the secondary server.

3. **Restore**: The transaction log is restored on the secondary server, which can then be used for reporting or recovery purposes.

Benefits:

- **Simplicity**: Log shipping is relatively simple to configure.

- **Recovery**: If the primary server fails, the secondary server can be brought online manually by restoring the last log backup.

Limitations:

- Requires manual intervention to bring the secondary server online after a failure.

- Does not support **automatic failover**.

2.3. Replication

SQL Server Replication is a method for distributing data from one database (the **publisher**) to other databases (the **subscribers**). Replication can be used for **high availability**, **data distribution**, and **load balancing**. There are different types of replication in SQL Server:

- **Transactional Replication**: Replicates **changes in real time** as they occur on the publisher.

- **Merge Replication**: Allows changes to be made at both the publisher and subscribers, and changes are later synchronized.

- **Snapshot Replication**: Takes a **snapshot of the data** and applies it to the subscribers on a set schedule.

Replication Configuration:

1. **Configure the Publisher**: Specify the database and tables to be replicated.

2. **Set Up the Distributor**: The distributor stores the replication data.

3. **Configure the Subscriber**: The subscribers receive the replicated data.

3. Failover Clustering and Disaster Recovery Planning

3.1. Failover Clustering in SQL Server

SQL Server Failover Clustering provides **high availability** by ensuring that, in the event of a failure, the workload can be moved to another node in the cluster. It is different from Always On AGs in that it operates at the **instance level** rather than the **database level**.

How Failover Clustering Works:

1. **Clustered Nodes**: A failover cluster consists of multiple **nodes** (physical or virtual machines) connected to shared storage.

2. **Failover Process**: If one node fails, the SQL Server instance can **failover** to another node in the cluster. This failover happens at the **instance level**.

3. **Clustered SQL Server Instance**: SQL Server is installed on all nodes in the cluster, and the cluster manager ensures the active node is always available.

Best Practices:

- Use **shared storage** (e.g., SAN or NAS) for storing SQL Server database files.

- Regularly test failover to ensure smooth operation during actual failures.

3.2. Disaster Recovery Planning

Disaster recovery (DR) planning is crucial for ensuring that your SQL Server environment can recover from major outages, including hardware failures, network issues, and natural disasters.

Key Components of a Disaster Recovery Plan:

1. **RPO and RTO**:

   o **Recovery Point Objective (RPO)**: The maximum allowable data loss (e.g., how much data you are willing to lose in the event of a failure).

   o **Recovery Time Objective (RTO)**: The maximum amount of time it should take to recover from a failure.

2. **Data Redundancy**: Use solutions like **Always On AGs**, **log shipping**, or **replication** to ensure data redundancy across multiple servers or locations.

3. **Offsite Backups**: Store backups at a remote site to ensure recovery in case of a **data center failure**.

Example DR Scenario:

- Implement **Always On AGs** for high availability.

- Use **log shipping** for offsite disaster recovery.

- Regularly test **failover scenarios** to ensure RTO and RPO goals are met.

4. Testing and Automating DR Scenarios

4.1. Testing High Availability and Disaster Recovery

Regular testing of your HA/DR solutions is critical to ensure that they will function properly when an actual failure occurs. Testing should be conducted during planned maintenance windows.

Testing Failover:

- Test **automatic failover** in Always On Availability Groups.

- Manually failover to ensure proper operation and validate data synchronization.

- Test **failover clustering** to verify instance-level failover.

Testing Database Recovery:

- Test **log shipping** by restoring logs to the secondary server.

- Test **replication** by simulating failure and ensuring replication continues without data loss.

Best Practices for Testing:

- Test **disaster recovery scenarios** at least once a year.

- Document **failure recovery procedures** to ensure consistency and efficiency.

4.2. Automating Disaster Recovery

Automation can help reduce human error and improve response times during DR events.

Using PowerShell for Automated Failover:

PowerShell scripts can be used to automate failover in Always On AGs or to trigger the restoration of log backups during log shipping.

Automated Monitoring and Alerts:

- Use **SQL Server Agent** to automate monitoring and trigger alerts based on specific conditions (e.g., primary replica failure, replication lag, etc.).

- Integrate with tools like **System Center** to provide a comprehensive DR monitoring system.

Chapter 8: High Availability and Disaster Recovery (HA/DR) Solutions

In today's world, data is a critical asset for businesses of all sizes. For SQL Server environments, ensuring **high availability (HA)** and **disaster recovery (DR)** is essential to safeguard against system failures, data loss, and prolonged downtime. Having a **comprehensive HA/DR solution** enables organizations to continue operating even in the face of hardware failures, software issues, or natural disasters.

In this chapter, we will delve into SQL Server's **High Availability** and **Disaster Recovery (HA/DR)** solutions. We will explore several strategies to ensure your SQL Server environment is **always available** and that you can **recover data quickly** when an outage occurs. The key solutions discussed will include:

- **SQL Server Always On Availability Groups**

- **Database Mirroring, Log Shipping, and Replication**

- **Failover Clustering and Disaster Recovery Planning**

- **Testing and Automating DR Scenarios**

By the end of this chapter, you will understand how to implement **robust HA/DR strategies** that ensure **data availability** and **business continuity**.

1. SQL Server Always On Availability Groups

1.1. Overview of Always On Availability Groups

Introduced in SQL Server 2012, **Always On Availability Groups** (AGs) offer a highly available and disaster-tolerant solution that allows **multiple copies of a database** (called **availability replicas**) to be synchronized across different servers. With AGs, you can achieve **automatic failover** and **data redundancy** with minimal downtime.

Key Features of Always On AGs:

- **Multiple replicas**: Support for up to **eight replicas** of a database.

- **Automatic failover**: When the primary replica fails, the secondary replica automatically takes over.

- **Readable secondary replicas**: Allow read-only workloads to be offloaded to secondary replicas.

- **Support for different availability modes**: **Synchronous** and **Asynchronous**.

Architecture of Always On AGs:

- **Primary Replica**: The primary replica is the read-write database instance that handles all client connections.

- **Secondary Replicas**: These are the standby instances that store copies of the database. In **synchronous** mode, the data is replicated in real time; in **asynchronous** mode, the replication happens with a lag.

- **Availability Group Listener**: A virtual network name that clients use to connect to the availability group, which points to the current primary replica.

1.2. Configuring Always On Availability Groups

To implement Always On AGs, certain prerequisites must be met, including setting up **Windows Server Failover Clustering** (WSFC) and ensuring that **SQL Server Enterprise Edition** is used. The following steps outline the process of configuring Always On AGs:

Step 1: Enable Always On AGs on SQL Server

1. Open **SQL Server Configuration Manager**.

2. Under **SQL Server Services**, right-click the **SQL Server** instance and select **Properties**.

3. Under the **Always On High Availability** tab, enable **Always On Availability Groups** and restart SQL Server.

Step 2: Set Up Windows Server Failover Cluster

1. Create a **Windows Server Failover Cluster** (WSFC) to manage failover capabilities.

2. Ensure that the cluster nodes are running **Windows Server 2012 or higher**.

3. Use **Cluster Manager** to validate the cluster configuration.

Step 3: Configure the Availability Group

1. Use **SQL Server Management Studio (SSMS)** to create an availability group.

2. Specify the **primary database**, choose the **secondary replicas**, and configure the **failover mode** (synchronous or asynchronous).

3. Set up the **availability group listener**, which will manage client redirection to the primary replica during failovers.

Step 4: Synchronize the Databases

Once the availability group is set up, SQL Server will begin **synchronizing** the database between the primary and secondary replicas. You can use **synchronous-commit mode** for real-time data replication or **asynchronous-commit mode** if a slight data lag is acceptable.

1.3. Managing Always On Availability Groups

Managing Always On AGs involves monitoring replica health, synchronizing databases, and handling failover events. Some key tasks include:

- **Monitoring Replica Health**: Always On Availability Groups can be monitored using **SQL Server Management Studio (SSMS), Dynamic Management Views (DMVs)**, and **SQL Server Profiler**.

- **Manual Failover**: In situations where the primary replica needs to be manually failed over (e.g., for maintenance), administrators can initiate a **planned failover** from SSMS.

- **Backup Strategies for AGs**: Always On supports backup operations from either the **primary replica** or **secondary replica** (for read-only workloads). It is recommended to back up the database from the secondary replica to reduce load on the primary replica.

2. Database Mirroring, Log Shipping, and Replication

While Always On Availability Groups are a powerful HA/DR solution, other methods like **database mirroring**, **log shipping**, and **replication** have been used for years and are still viable options depending on your organization's needs.

2.1. Database Mirroring

Database Mirroring is a high-availability solution that maintains two copies of a database: a **primary** and a **mirror**. Mirroring can be configured to work in either **synchronous** or

asynchronous modes. It is important to note that Microsoft is **deprecating database mirroring** in favor of Always On AGs.

Configuration Steps:

1. **Set Up Principal and Mirror Instances**: The principal database is the primary source of data, and the mirror database is an exact copy of the principal.

2. **Configure the Witness Server**: The witness server helps in automatic failover by monitoring the health of the principal server.

3. **Monitor Mirroring**: Use **SQL Server Management Studio** to monitor the status of database mirroring.

2.2. Log Shipping

Log Shipping is a disaster recovery solution where **transaction log backups** from the primary database are automatically copied to a secondary server. These log backups are then applied to the secondary server.

How Log Shipping Works:

1. **Backup**: A transaction log backup is taken from the primary server at regular intervals.

2. **Copy**: The log backup is copied to the secondary server.

3. **Restore**: The transaction log is restored on the secondary server, which can then be used for reporting or recovery purposes.

Benefits:

- **Simplicity**: Log shipping is relatively simple to configure.

- **Recovery**: If the primary server fails, the secondary server can be brought online manually by restoring the last log backup.

Limitations:

- Requires manual intervention to bring the secondary server online after a failure.

- Does not support **automatic failover**.

2.3. Replication

SQL Server Replication is a method for distributing data from one database (the **publisher**) to other databases (the **subscribers**). Replication can be used for **high availability**, **data distribution**, and **load balancing**. There are different types of replication in SQL Server:

- **Transactional Replication**: Replicates **changes in real time** as they occur on the publisher.

- **Merge Replication**: Allows changes to be made at both the publisher and subscribers, and changes are later synchronized.

- **Snapshot Replication**: Takes a **snapshot of the data** and applies it to the subscribers on a set schedule.

Replication Configuration:

1. **Configure the Publisher**: Specify the database and tables to be replicated.

2. **Set Up the Distributor**: The distributor stores the replication data.

3. **Configure the Subscriber**: The subscribers receive the replicated data.

3. Failover Clustering and Disaster Recovery Planning

3.1. Failover Clustering in SQL Server

SQL Server Failover Clustering provides **high availability** by ensuring that, in the event of a failure, the workload can be moved to another node in the cluster. It is different from Always On AGs in that it operates at the **instance level** rather than the **database level**.

How Failover Clustering Works:

1. **Clustered Nodes**: A failover cluster consists of multiple **nodes** (physical or virtual machines) connected to shared storage.

2. **Failover Process**: If one node fails, the SQL Server instance can **failover** to another node in the cluster. This failover happens at the **instance level**.

3. **Clustered SQL Server Instance**: SQL Server is installed on all nodes in the cluster, and the cluster manager ensures the active node is always available.

Best Practices:

- Use **shared storage** (e.g., SAN or NAS) for storing SQL Server database files.

- Regularly test failover to ensure smooth operation during actual failures.

3.2. Disaster Recovery Planning

Disaster recovery (DR) planning is crucial for ensuring that your SQL Server environment can recover from major outages, including hardware failures, network issues, and natural disasters.

Key Components of a Disaster Recovery Plan:

1. **RPO and RTO**:

   - **Recovery Point Objective (RPO)**: The maximum allowable data loss (e.g., how much data you are willing to lose in the event of a failure).

   - **Recovery Time Objective (RTO)**: The maximum amount of time it should take to recover from a failure.

2. **Data Redundancy**: Use solutions like **Always On AGs**, **log shipping**, or **replication** to ensure data redundancy across multiple servers or locations.

3. **Offsite Backups**: Store backups at a remote site to ensure recovery in case of a **data center failure**.

Example DR Scenario:

- Implement **Always On AGs** for high availability.

- Use **log shipping** for offsite disaster recovery.

- Regularly test **failover scenarios** to ensure RTO and RPO goals are met.

4. Testing and Automating DR Scenarios

4.1. Testing High Availability and Disaster Recovery

Regular testing of your HA/DR solutions is critical to ensure that they will function properly when an actual failure occurs. Testing should be conducted during planned maintenance windows.

Testing Failover:

- Test **automatic failover** in Always On Availability Groups.

- Manually failover to ensure proper operation and validate data synchronization.

- Test **failover clustering** to verify instance-level failover.

Testing Database Recovery:

- Test **log shipping** by restoring logs to the secondary server.

- Test **replication** by simulating failure and ensuring replication continues without data loss.

Best Practices for Testing:

- Test **disaster recovery scenarios** at least once a year.

- Document **failure recovery procedures** to ensure consistency and efficiency.

4.2. Automating Disaster Recovery

Automation can help reduce human error and improve response times during DR events.

Using PowerShell for Automated Failover:

PowerShell scripts can be used to automate failover in Always On AGs or to trigger the restoration of log backups during log shipping.

Automated Monitoring and Alerts:

- Use **SQL Server Agent** to automate monitoring and trigger alerts based on specific conditions (e.g., primary replica failure, replication lag, etc.).

- Integrate with tools like **System Center** to provide a comprehensive DR monitoring system.

Chapter 9: SQL Server Performance Monitoring and Troubleshooting

SQL Server performance monitoring and troubleshooting are crucial tasks for database administrators (DBAs) to ensure that the database is running efficiently and is able to handle growing workloads. Performance bottlenecks, slow queries, and deadlocks are common issues that can hinder database operations and affect user experience. The ability to effectively **monitor performance, identify issues**, and **troubleshoot** them in a timely manner is critical for maintaining system health.

This chapter will cover the following topics:

- **Identifying and Resolving Performance Bottlenecks**

- **Using Performance Monitor, Extended Events, and Profiler**

- **Troubleshooting Slow Queries and Deadlocks**

- **Proactive Monitoring with SQL Server Agent Alerts**

By the end of this chapter, you will have the tools and techniques necessary to **optimize SQL Server performance**, resolve common issues, and ensure smooth operation of your database environment.

1. Identifying and Resolving Performance Bottlenecks

Performance bottlenecks occur when a system's capacity is exceeded in one or more areas, leading to delays or degraded performance. These bottlenecks may appear in the **CPU, memory, disk I/O**, or **network** layers. Identifying and resolving these bottlenecks is essential for keeping SQL Server running optimally.

1.1. Common Performance Bottlenecks

1. **CPU Bottlenecks**:

   o **Symptoms**: High CPU usage, slow response times, and processes waiting for CPU resources.

   o **Causes**: Long-running queries, complex joins, or inefficient queries consuming excessive CPU time.

   o **Solution**:

      ▪ Optimize queries by reducing the use of **subqueries, joins**, and **unnecessary operations**.

- Use **indexing** to speed up data retrieval.

- Check for missing **statistics** or **indexes** that may be causing inefficient execution plans.

- Monitor CPU usage using **SQL Server Profiler** and **Performance Monitor**.

2. **Memory Bottlenecks**:

   o **Symptoms**: High memory usage, SQL Server crashing or slow performance during large data operations.

   o **Causes**: Memory allocation by SQL Server exceeding available system memory, causing paging.

   o **Solution**:

       - Configure **max server memory** to ensure SQL Server does not consume all available memory.

       - Use **Resource Governor** to allocate specific memory resources to workloads.

- Monitor memory usage via **Dynamic Management Views (DMVs)** like sys.dm_os_memory_clerks.

3. **Disk I/O Bottlenecks**:

   o **Symptoms**: Slow response times during data retrieval, high latency in reads/writes, or resource contention.

   o **Causes**: Poor disk subsystem performance, lack of proper disk configuration, or high query volume.

   o **Solution**:

     - Use **SSD drives** for faster data reads and writes.

     - Configure **multiple data files** for tempdb and data files to distribute I/O load.

     - Monitor disk activity using **Performance Monitor** and **sys.dm_io_virtual_file_stats** DMV.

4. **Network Bottlenecks**:

- Symptoms: Slow performance during remote connections or long wait times for remote queries.

- Causes: Network latency, high network traffic, or inefficient network configurations.

- Solution:

  - Use **Connection Pooling** to reduce the overhead of opening and closing connections.

  - Ensure the network bandwidth is sufficient for the load.

  - Monitor network performance using **Performance Monitor** and system tools.

1.2. Tools to Identify Bottlenecks

Several tools are available within SQL Server to identify and resolve performance bottlenecks. These tools help DBAs to diagnose the root cause of performance degradation and address it.

Performance Monitor (PerfMon)

Performance Monitor is a built-in tool in Windows that can track the performance of SQL Server instances. It provides real-time data for several system metrics that are critical for SQL Server performance, including:

- **Processor Time**: Monitors the percentage of CPU being used by SQL Server.

- **Memory Usage**: Monitors SQL Server memory consumption, including page life expectancy and buffer cache hit ratios.

- **Disk I/O**: Tracks read/write operations for SQL Server data files.

- **SQL Server:SQL Statistics**: Provides information on SQL Server wait times and cache hit ratios.

Using **Performance Monitor**, you can identify areas with high resource consumption and focus your troubleshooting efforts on those components.

Dynamic Management Views (DMVs)

SQL Server includes a number of **DMVs** that help DBAs identify performance bottlenecks. Some key DMVs include:

- **sys.dm_exec_requests**: Displays information about current SQL Server requests, including CPU time, disk I/O, and blocking.

- **sys.dm_exec_query_stats**: Displays statistics about query execution times and resource usage.

- **sys.dm_os_wait_stats**: Provides information about the types of waits that SQL Server has experienced, which can help identify resource contention issues.

These views can be queried to pinpoint the areas where SQL Server is encountering performance issues.

2. Using Performance Monitor, Extended Events, and Profiler

2.1. Performance Monitor

Performance Monitor allows DBAs to track the real-time performance of SQL Server and underlying hardware. By monitoring key performance counters, DBAs can quickly identify resource contention or inefficiencies. Common **SQL Server performance counters** to monitor include:

- **SQLServer:Buffer Manager**:

  o Buffer cache hit ratio: Measures how often pages are found in the buffer cache.

  o Page life expectancy: Indicates how long a page stays in memory.

- **SQLServer:SQL Statistics**:

  o SQL Compilations/sec: The rate at which SQL Server compiles queries.

  o SQL Re-Compilations/sec: The rate at which SQL Server recompiles queries due to plan cache invalidation.

- **SQLServer:Databases**:

  o Log Cache Hit Ratio: Indicates how efficiently log writes are processed.

  o Log Flushes/sec: The rate at which transaction logs are flushed to disk.

By analyzing these counters, DBAs can identify trends that indicate performance bottlenecks and take corrective action.

2.2. Extended Events

Extended Events are a powerful monitoring tool for diagnosing SQL Server performance problems. They provide a lightweight way to capture detailed event data about various SQL Server activities. Unlike **SQL Profiler**, Extended Events have a much lower performance overhead, making them ideal for troubleshooting in production environments.

Key Extended Events for Performance Monitoring:

- **Query Execution Events**: Capture information about query performance, including execution times and resource usage.

- **Locking and Blocking Events**: Track instances of **blocking** and **deadlocks**.

- **Wait Events**: Capture wait statistics to help identify resource contention issues.

To create an Extended Event session for monitoring query performance, you can use the following code:

sql

```sql
CREATE EVENT SESSION QueryPerformance

ON SERVER

ADD EVENT sqlserver.sql_batch_completed

( ACTION (sqlserver.sql_text, sqlserver.database_name)

WHERE (duration > 1000000) )

ADD TARGET package0.ring_buffer;

GO

ALTER EVENT SESSION QueryPerformance

ON SERVER STATE = START;
```

This session will capture all queries that take longer than 1 second to complete, which can help identify performance bottlenecks related to specific queries.

2.3. SQL Profiler

SQL Profiler is a legacy tool that allows DBAs to capture and analyze SQL Server activity in real time. Although it can add significant overhead to the server, it remains useful for troubleshooting slow queries or capturing detailed information about SQL Server operations.

Using SQL Profiler:

1. Open **SQL Server Profiler** from SSMS.

2. Create a new **Trace** and select events such as **SQL:BatchCompleted**, **RPC:Completed**, and **Deadlock Graph**.

3. Specify filters to limit the amount of data captured (e.g., only queries from a specific database).

4. Analyze the trace for long-running queries, deadlocks, or resource-intensive operations.

While **Profiler** is useful, it is generally recommended to use **Extended Events** for production environments due to their lower overhead.

3. Troubleshooting Slow Queries and Deadlocks

3.1. Troubleshooting Slow Queries

Slow queries are a common source of performance issues in SQL Server environments. The root causes of slow queries can range from inefficient SQL code to lack of proper indexing. To troubleshoot slow queries, follow these steps:

1. **Check the Execution Plan**:

   o Use **SQL Server Management Studio (SSMS)** to view the **query execution plan**. Look for operations that are consuming excessive CPU, memory, or disk I/O.

   o Common issues include missing indexes, inefficient joins, or table scans.

2. **Optimize Indexing**:

   o Identify missing or fragmented indexes using **DMVs** such as sys.dm_db_index_physical_stats and sys.dm_db_missing_index_details.

- Consider adding appropriate **non-clustered indexes** for frequently queried columns.

3. **Analyze Wait Statistics**:

   - Use sys.dm_os_wait_stats to identify what SQL Server is waiting for. Common waits include **CXPACKET** (parallelism issues) or **PAGEIOLATCH** (disk I/O issues).

4. **Query Tuning**:

   - Review the query for inefficiencies. Avoid using **SELECT *** in production queries and ensure that only necessary columns are retrieved.

   - Use **Table Variables** and **CTEs** wisely, and avoid excessive nesting of queries.

3.2. Troubleshooting Deadlocks

A **deadlock** occurs when two or more processes are blocking each other by holding locks on resources that the other processes need. SQL Server automatically detects deadlocks and will terminate one of the transactions to resolve the situation. However, frequent deadlocks can impact performance and should be minimized.

Steps to Troubleshoot Deadlocks:

1. **Capture Deadlock Graphs**:

   o Use **SQL Profiler** or **Extended Events** to capture **Deadlock Graph** events. The deadlock graph provides detailed information about the involved processes and resources.

2. **Analyze the Deadlock**:

   o Review the **deadlock graph** to identify which resources and processes are involved in the deadlock.

   o Identify patterns in the deadlock, such as specific queries, tables, or application code that are consistently involved.

3. **Resolve the Deadlock**:

   o **Optimize the queries** involved in the deadlock by adding indexes or modifying the query structure.

- Minimize transaction duration by reducing the amount of time locks are held on resources.

- Consider using **row-level locking** or **optimizing transaction isolation levels** to reduce lock contention.

4. Proactive Monitoring with SQL Server Agent Alerts

4.1. Configuring SQL Server Agent Alerts

SQL Server Agent is a powerful tool that allows DBAs to automate and monitor SQL Server tasks. One of the key features of SQL Server Agent is **Alerts**, which can notify administrators about specific performance or error conditions.

Common Alerts to Set Up:

- **SQL Server Error Log**: Alert when specific errors occur in the SQL Server error log.

- **Performance Conditions**: Set up alerts to monitor CPU, memory, disk, or query performance thresholds.

- **Job Failures**: Monitor the success or failure of SQL Server jobs such as backups or index maintenance.

Creating an Alert:

1. Open **SQL Server Management Studio (SSMS)**.

2. In **SQL Server Agent**, navigate to **Alerts** and create a new alert.

3. Define the **condition** for the alert (e.g., a specific error number or performance counter threshold).

4. Specify the **response** (e.g., send an email notification, execute a job).

PART 4: ADVANCED ADMINISTRATION, AUTOMATION, AND CLOUD INTEGRATION

Chapter 10: Automating Database Administration Tasks

Database administrators (DBAs) are responsible for ensuring the efficient operation, security, and maintenance of SQL Server environments. However, many database administration tasks—such as backups, index maintenance, job monitoring, and data integration—are repetitive and time-consuming. By implementing **automation**, DBAs can significantly reduce manual effort, minimize human errors, and improve database performance.

SQL Server provides multiple tools for automation, including:

- **SQL Server Agent Jobs and Alerts** – Automating routine tasks like backups and performance monitoring.

- **PowerShell Scripting** – Using PowerShell to manage SQL Server at scale.

- **SQL Server Integration Services (SSIS)** – Automating data integration and ETL processes.

- **Maintenance Plans and Index Rebuilds** – Ensuring database performance remains optimal through automated maintenance.

This chapter will explore these techniques in detail, providing practical implementation strategies to help DBAs streamline their workflows.

1. SQL Server Agent Jobs and Alerts

1.1. Understanding SQL Server Agent

SQL Server Agent is a built-in scheduling and automation tool in SQL Server that allows DBAs to automate administrative tasks such as backups, data imports, monitoring, and job scheduling.

Key Benefits of SQL Server Agent:

✅ **Task Scheduling** – Run database tasks at predefined intervals.

✅ **Automated Monitoring** – Detect and respond to database issues automatically.

✅ **Error Handling** – Set up alerts for job failures.

✅ **Security Control** – Run tasks under different security contexts.

1.2. Configuring SQL Server Agent Jobs

A **SQL Server Agent job** consists of one or more steps that execute SQL scripts, stored procedures, or external applications.

Step 1: Enabling SQL Server Agent

SQL Server Agent is disabled by default in some editions. To enable it:

1. Open **SQL Server Configuration Manager**.

2. Locate **SQL Server Agent** and set the **Startup Type** to **Automatic**.

3. Start the **SQL Server Agent service**.

Step 2: Creating a SQL Server Agent Job

1. Open **SQL Server Management Studio (SSMS)**.

2. Expand **SQL Server Agent > Jobs**.

3. Right-click **Jobs** and select **New Job**.

4. Enter a **job name** and select an appropriate **owner** (such as sa).

5. Click on the **Steps** page and **Add a new step**.

6. Choose **Transact-SQL script (T-SQL)** as the job type.

7. Enter the SQL script (e.g., a database backup command):

sql

CopyEdit

BACKUP DATABASE MyDatabase TO DISK = 'C:\Backups\MyDatabase.bak' WITH FORMAT, INIT;

8. Click **OK**, then go to the **Schedules** tab to define a job schedule (e.g., daily at midnight).

9. Click **OK** to save the job.

1.3. Setting Up SQL Server Agent Alerts

SQL Server Agent **alerts** notify DBAs when specific conditions occur, such as a job failure, high CPU usage, or a full transaction log.

Step 1: Configuring Database Mail for Alerts

To receive email alerts, configure **Database Mail**:

sql

```
EXEC msdb.dbo.sp_send_dbmail

    @profile_name = 'AdminProfile',

    @recipients = 'dba@example.com',

    @subject = 'SQL Server Alert',

    @body = 'A SQL Server alert has been triggered.';
```

Step 2: Creating an Alert for Job Failures

1. In SSMS, expand **SQL Server Agent > Alerts**.

2. Right-click **Alerts** and select **New Alert**.

3. Choose **SQL Server Event Alert**.

4. Set **Error Number** to 9002 (for transaction log full errors).

5. In the **Response** tab, select **Notify Operators** and configure an email recipient.

6. Click **OK** to save the alert.

Best Practice: Configure alerts for **high CPU usage, failed backups, and deadlocks**.

2. PowerShell Scripting for SQL Server

2.1. Introduction to SQL Server PowerShell (SQLPS)

PowerShell provides powerful scripting capabilities for automating SQL Server administration. The **SQLServer PowerShell module** allows DBAs to perform database operations programmatically.

Benefits of Using PowerShell for SQL Server:

✓ **Automate repetitive tasks** like backups and index maintenance.

✓ **Manage multiple SQL Servers** from a single script.

✓ **Integrate with Windows Task Scheduler** for automation.

2.2. Automating Common SQL Server Tasks with PowerShell

Automating Database Backup

powershell

```
Backup-SqlDatabase -ServerInstance "SQLServerName" -
Database "MyDatabase" -BackupFile
"C:\Backups\MyDatabase.bak"
```

Retrieving a List of Running Queries

powershell

```
Invoke-Sqlcmd -ServerInstance "SQLServerName" -Database
"master" -Query "SELECT * FROM sys.dm_exec_requests"
```

Index Maintenance with PowerShell

powershell

```
Invoke-Sqlcmd -ServerInstance "SQLServerName" -Database
"MyDatabase" -Query "ALTER INDEX ALL ON MyTable
REBUILD"
```

Best Practice: Use **PowerShell scripts with SQL Server Agent** for scheduled automation.

3. Using SSIS for Data Integration and Automation

3.1. What is SQL Server Integration Services (SSIS)?

SSIS (SQL Server Integration Services) is a Microsoft tool for **automating data integration, ETL (Extract, Transform, Load), and data migration**.

Key SSIS Features:

✅ **Automate Data Imports** from files, databases, or APIs.

✅ **Transform Data** using ETL processes.

✅ **Schedule Data Transfers** using SQL Server Agent.

3.2. Automating Data Import with SSIS

Step 1: Create an SSIS Package for Data Import

1. Open **SQL Server Data Tools (SSDT)**.

2. Create a new **Integration Services Project**.

3. Drag a **Data Flow Task** onto the workspace.

4. Configure a **Flat File Source** (e.g., C:\data\import.csv).

5. Add an **OLE DB Destination** and connect it to a **SQL Server table**.

6. Run the package to test the data import.

Step 2: Scheduling the SSIS Package in SQL Server Agent

1. In SSMS, expand **SQL Server Agent > Jobs**.

2. Create a new job and add a step of type **SQL Server Integration Services Package**.

3. Choose the SSIS package and set up a schedule.

Best Practice: Monitor SSIS execution using **Event Handlers** to catch errors.

4. Automating Maintenance Plans and Index Rebuilds

4.1. Automating Database Maintenance Plans

SQL Server provides built-in **Maintenance Plans** to automate tasks like backups, index rebuilding, and integrity checks.

Creating a Maintenance Plan for Backups

1. Open **SSMS**, go to **Management > Maintenance Plans**.

2. Right-click and select **New Maintenance Plan**.

3. Add a **Backup Database Task**.

4. Configure a schedule to run **daily at 2 AM**.

5. Click **OK** to save.

4.2. Automating Index Maintenance

Rebuilding Indexes Automatically

sql

```
ALTER INDEX ALL ON MyTable REBUILD;
```

Scheduling Index Maintenance

1. Create a **SQL Server Agent Job**.

2. Add a step with the above SQL command.

3. Schedule it to run **weekly**.

Best Practice: Monitor index fragmentation with:

sql

```sql
SELECT * FROM sys.dm_db_index_physical_stats(DB_ID(),
NULL, NULL, NULL, 'DETAILED');
```

Chapter 11: Advanced Query Optimization and Execution Plan Analysis

Efficient query execution is crucial for maintaining **high performance and scalability** in SQL Server databases. Poorly optimized queries can lead to **slow response times, excessive CPU and memory usage, and blocked transactions**, ultimately affecting application performance. Understanding **execution plans, parameter sniffing, query hints, plan guides, and query wait times** is essential for tuning queries and ensuring optimal database performance.

This chapter explores **advanced techniques** for optimizing queries and analyzing execution plans. We will cover:

- **Understanding Execution Plans and Query Optimization Techniques**

- **Parameter Sniffing, Query Hints, and Plan Guides**

- **Analyzing and Reducing Query Wait Times**

- **Using Database Engine Tuning Advisor**

By the end of this chapter, you will be able to **interpret execution plans, optimize slow queries, reduce performance bottlenecks**, and leverage SQL Server's built-in tools for performance tuning.

1. Understanding Execution Plans and Query Optimization Techniques

1.1. What is an Execution Plan?

An **execution plan** is a detailed breakdown of how SQL Server **executes a query**. It shows the **order of operations**, the **indexes used**, and the **estimated vs. actual query costs**. Understanding execution plans allows DBAs and developers to **identify inefficient query patterns** and optimize them for better performance.

Why Execution Plans Matter:

✓ Help in detecting **table scans and missing indexes**

✓ Show **query cost estimates** for performance evaluation

✅ Help diagnose **inefficient join operations**

✅ Provide insights into **parallel query execution and resource usage**

1.2. Types of Execution Plans

SQL Server provides two types of execution plans:

1. **Estimated Execution Plan**

   o Displays a **predicted** query plan without actually executing the query.

   o Useful for **query planning** and detecting **potential inefficiencies**.

   o Generated using CTRL + L in SSMS or via:

sql

```
SET SHOWPLAN_XML ON;

GO

SELECT * FROM Orders WHERE OrderDate > '2024-01-01';
```

GO

SET SHOWPLAN_XML OFF;

2. **Actual Execution Plan**

   o Shows the **real execution path** taken by SQL
   Server.

   o Includes **actual row counts, CPU time**, and
   disk I/O statistics.

   o Generated by executing the query with CTRL +
   M in SSMS.

1.3. How to Read an Execution Plan

Execution plans contain multiple **operators**, each representing
a step in the query execution process. Some common operators
include:

- **Table Scan** – Reads all rows from a table (inefficient).

- **Clustered Index Scan** – Scans the entire clustered
  index.

- **Clustered Index Seek** – Efficiently retrieves data using an index.

- **Nested Loops Join** – Good for small datasets but inefficient for large ones.

- **Hash Join** – Used for joining large tables efficiently.

Example: Detecting a Table Scan

sql

```
SELECT * FROM Customers WHERE LastName = 'Smith';
```

If no index exists on LastName, SQL Server will perform a **table scan**, leading to poor performance.

✅ **Solution:** Create an index:

sql

```
CREATE INDEX idx_LastName ON Customers (LastName);
```

2. Parameter Sniffing, Query Hints, and Plan Guides

2.1. What is Parameter Sniffing?

Parameter sniffing occurs when SQL Server **reuses a cached execution plan** based on the first parameter value encountered. While this can improve performance, it can also lead to **suboptimal query plans** when data distribution varies significantly.

Example of Parameter Sniffing Issue:

sql

CREATE PROCEDURE GetOrdersByCustomer

(@CustomerID INT)

AS

SELECT * FROM Orders WHERE CustomerID = @CustomerID;

If the stored procedure is executed first with @CustomerID = 1 (a small dataset), SQL Server may create a **query plan optimized for a small number of rows**. When the same plan is used for @CustomerID = 10000 (a large dataset), performance may degrade.

✅ **Solutions to Parameter Sniffing:**

- **Use OPTION (RECOMPILE)** to force a new execution plan for each execution:

sql

SELECT * FROM Orders WHERE CustomerID = @CustomerID OPTION (RECOMPILE);

- **Use Local Variables** to prevent SQL Server from sniffing parameter values:

sql

DECLARE @LocalCustomerID INT = @CustomerID;

SELECT * FROM Orders WHERE CustomerID = @LocalCustomerID;

2.2. Using Query Hints for Performance Optimization

Query hints **override SQL Server's default optimization behavior**, allowing DBAs to manually influence execution plans.

Common Query Hints:

Query Hint	Description
OPTION (RECOMPILE)	Forces SQL Server to generate a new execution plan each time.
FORCESEEK	Forces SQL Server to use an **index seek** instead of a scan.
LOOP JOIN	Forces a **nested loops join**.
HASH JOIN	Forces a **hash join**, useful for large tables.

Example: Using FORCESEEK to Optimize Index Usage

sql

```
SELECT * FROM Customers WHERE LastName = 'Smith'
OPTION (FORCESEEK);
```

2.3. Plan Guides: Controlling Execution Plans

Plan guides allow DBAs to **modify query execution plans** without changing application code.

Creating a Plan Guide:

sql

```
EXEC sp_create_plan_guide

    @name = N'OptimizeOrders',

    @stmt = N'SELECT * FROM Orders WHERE OrderDate > @OrderDate',

    @type = N'OBJECT',

    @module_or_batch = N'usp_GetRecentOrders',

    @params = NULL,

    @hints = N'OPTION (OPTIMIZE FOR UNKNOWN)';
```

This ensures the optimizer **ignores specific parameter values** when generating a plan.

3. Analyzing and Reducing Query Wait Times

3.1. Using Dynamic Management Views (DMVs) to Analyze Query Performance

SQL Server provides **DMVs** that help analyze query performance and wait times.

Checking Query Wait Statistics:

sql

```
SELECT wait_type, wait_time_ms, waiting_tasks_count
FROM sys.dm_os_wait_stats
ORDER BY wait_time_ms DESC;
```

Common Wait Types:

Wait Type	Description	Solution
CXPACKET	Parallelism wait (too many parallel threads).	Adjust MAXDOP setting.

PAGEIOLATCH	Slow disk I/O.	Use faster SSD storage.
LCK_M_X	Blocking due to locks.	Optimize transaction handling.

3.2. Identifying Long-Running Queries

To find slow queries:

sql

```
SELECT TOP 10 query_text, total_worker_time

FROM sys.dm_exec_query_stats

CROSS APPLY sys.dm_exec_sql_text(sql_handle)

ORDER BY total_worker_time DESC;
```

✅ **Solution:**

- Create **missing indexes**.

- Use **query tuning techniques** such as indexing and statistics updates.

- Analyze execution plans and **eliminate unnecessary table scans**.

4. Using Database Engine Tuning Advisor

4.1. What is Database Engine Tuning Advisor (DTA)?

DTA is a tool that helps DBAs optimize queries by recommending:

✅ **Index creation**

✅ **Partitioning strategies**

✅ **Statistics updates**

4.2. Running DTA for Performance Analysis

1. Open **SQL Server Management Studio (SSMS)**.

2. Navigate to **Tools > Database Engine Tuning Advisor**.

3. Select a **workload file** (or a query from SSMS).

4. Click **Start Analysis**.

5. Review **indexing and optimization recommendations**.

Chapter 12: SQL Server Integration with Cloud and Hybrid Environments

As organizations shift towards cloud computing, database management strategies must adapt to **hybrid and cloud-based environments**. SQL Server, a core component of enterprise data infrastructure, can now be deployed on **Azure, AWS, and Google Cloud**, as well as in hybrid architectures that combine **on-premises and cloud resources**. The ability to integrate SQL Server with cloud technologies offers **scalability, cost optimization, high availability, and performance enhancements**.

This chapter explores how SQL Server integrates with cloud and hybrid environments, covering:

- **SQL Server in Azure, AWS, and Google Cloud**

- **Azure SQL Database vs. Managed Instances**

- **Hybrid Cloud Strategies and Data Migration**

- **SQL Server and Kubernetes**

By the end of this chapter, you will understand **the different cloud options for SQL Server, best practices for hybrid deployments, and the role of Kubernetes in modern database management.**

1. SQL Server in Azure, AWS, and Google Cloud

SQL Server is supported on all major cloud platforms: **Microsoft Azure, Amazon Web Services (AWS), and Google Cloud Platform (GCP)**. Each cloud provider offers different **deployment models**, ranging from **virtual machines (VMs)** running SQL Server to **fully managed database services**.

1.1. SQL Server in Microsoft Azure

Azure SQL provides multiple deployment options for running SQL Server in the cloud, including:

- **Azure SQL Database** – A **fully managed** relational database service.

- **Azure SQL Managed Instance** – A **lift-and-shift solution** for migrating on-prem SQL Server workloads to Azure.

- **SQL Server on Azure Virtual Machines (VMs)** – Runs a **full SQL Server instance** on an Azure VM.

✅ **Benefits of SQL Server in Azure:**

- **Seamless integration** with other Microsoft cloud services.

- **Built-in security and compliance features** (e.g., Transparent Data Encryption).

- **Automatic scaling and performance tuning** using AI-driven insights.

1.2. SQL Server in AWS

AWS offers multiple options for deploying SQL Server:

- **Amazon RDS for SQL Server** – A fully managed **relational database service**.

- **SQL Server on EC2** – Runs SQL Server on an **AWS Virtual Machine (EC2 instance)**.

- **Amazon Aurora (SQL Server compatible)** – A cloud-native alternative with **high scalability**.

✅ **Benefits of SQL Server on AWS:**

- **High availability and automated backups.**

- **Multi-region replication for disaster recovery**.

- **Integration with AWS analytics and machine learning services**.

1.3. SQL Server in Google Cloud

Google Cloud provides SQL Server deployments through:

- **Cloud SQL for SQL Server** – A fully managed SQL Server database.

- **SQL Server on Compute Engine (VMs)** – Deploy SQL Server on Google Cloud VMs.

✅ **Benefits of SQL Server on Google Cloud:**

- **Competitive pricing and licensing flexibility**.

- **Built-in machine learning and analytics integration**.

- **Low-latency global networking**.

2. Azure SQL Database vs. Managed Instances

When migrating SQL Server to Azure, organizations must choose between **Azure SQL Database** and **Azure SQL Managed Instance**.

2.1. What is Azure SQL Database?

Azure SQL Database is a **fully managed, cloud-native relational database service** optimized for modern applications.

✓ **Key Features:**

- **Automatic backups, patching, and updates**.

- **Built-in AI-powered performance tuning**.

- **Elastic scalability with serverless options**.

- **Geo-replication for high availability**.

Best for: Cloud-first applications that require high availability and auto-scaling.

2.2. What is Azure SQL Managed Instance?

Azure SQL Managed Instance is designed for **migrating on-prem SQL Server workloads** to the cloud **with minimal code changes**.

✅ **Key Features:**

- **Full SQL Server feature compatibility**.

- **Supports SQL Agent, cross-database queries, and linked servers**.

- **Easier migration from on-prem SQL Server**.

- **Integrated VNET support for secure connections**.

🚀 **Best for: Lift-and-shift migrations** from on-prem SQL Server to Azure.

2.3. Choosing Between Azure SQL Database and Managed Instances

Feature	Azure SQL Database	Azure SQL Managed Instance

Fully Managed	✅ Yes	✅ Yes
SQL Agent Support	❌ No	✅ Yes
Linked Server Support	❌ No	✅ Yes
Geo-Replication	✅ Yes	✅ Yes
Ideal Use Case	Cloud-native apps	Lift-and-shift migrations

Best Practice: Use **Azure SQL Database** for **new applications** and **Managed Instance** for **on-prem migrations**.

3. Hybrid Cloud Strategies and Data Migration

Many enterprises operate in a **hybrid cloud** model, where SQL Server databases are **distributed across on-premises and cloud environments**. Hybrid strategies allow organizations to **gradually transition to the cloud** while maintaining control over **sensitive data** and ensuring **business continuity**.

3.1. Hybrid Cloud Architectures for SQL Server

A hybrid SQL Server deployment typically involves:

- **On-prem SQL Server with Cloud Disaster Recovery** – Keeping **primary databases on-prem** and **backups in the cloud**.

- **Cloud Read-Replicas for Reporting** – Running **real-time reporting workloads** on cloud-based SQL Server instances.

- **Active-Active Hybrid Deployment** – Using **geo-distributed SQL Server clusters** across on-prem and cloud environments.

✅ **Best Practice**: Use **Azure Hybrid Benefit** to reduce SQL Server licensing costs in hybrid deployments.

3.2. Data Migration Strategies

Migrating SQL Server to the cloud requires careful planning. The most common migration approaches are:

1. **Backup and Restore Method**

- Take a **full database backup** from on-prem SQL Server:

sql

```
BACKUP DATABASE MyDatabase TO DISK = 'C:\Backup\MyDatabase.bak';
```

- Upload the backup to **Azure Blob Storage or AWS S3**.

- Restore the backup to a cloud SQL Server instance:

sql

```
RESTORE DATABASE MyDatabase FROM DISK = '/cloudstorage/MyDatabase.bak';
```

2. **Azure Database Migration Service (DMS)**

- Automates **online and offline** migrations from on-prem SQL Server to Azure.

- Supports **schema conversion** and **real-time data replication**.

3. **Transactional Replication**

   - Ideal for **minimal downtime migrations**.

   - Replicates **on-prem data to a cloud SQL Server** in near real-time.

🚀 **Best Practice**: Use **DMS** for full migrations and **replication** for live migrations with minimal downtime.

4. SQL Server and Kubernetes

4.1. Running SQL Server in Kubernetes

Kubernetes is a **container orchestration platform** that allows SQL Server to run in a **scalable, portable environment**. **SQL Server on Kubernetes** is commonly deployed using:

- **Azure Kubernetes Service (AKS)**

- **Amazon Elastic Kubernetes Service (EKS)**

- **Google Kubernetes Engine (GKE)**

4.2. Deploying SQL Server on Kubernetes

Step 1: Create a Kubernetes Deployment File

yaml

```
apiVersion: apps/v1
kind: Deployment
metadata:
  name: sqlserver
spec:
  replicas: 1
  selector:
    matchLabels:
      app: sqlserver
  template:
    metadata:
```

```
    labels:

      app: sqlserver

  spec:

    containers:

    - name: sqlserver

      image: mcr.microsoft.com/mssql/server:2019-latest

      ports:

      - containerPort: 1433
```

Step 2: Deploy SQL Server to Kubernetes

sh

```
kubectl apply -f sqlserver-deployment.yaml
```

🚀 **Best Practice**: Use **Persistent Volumes (PVs)** to store SQL Server data across Kubernetes pod restarts.

Chapter 13: Database Replication and Data Synchronization Strategies

Database replication is a critical feature in SQL Server that ensures **data consistency, high availability, and scalability** across multiple databases and locations. Organizations that operate **distributed systems, cloud-based applications, or high-traffic workloads** rely on replication to synchronize data across different servers.

SQL Server offers **multiple replication strategies**, including **Transactional Replication, Merge Replication, and Snapshot Replication**, each suited for different **business requirements**. Proper replication management ensures that **data remains synchronized, queries run efficiently, and system failures do not result in data loss**.

This chapter explores:

- **Overview of SQL Server Replication Types**

- **Configuring and Managing Transactional Replication**

- **Data Synchronization Techniques for Distributed Databases**

- **Troubleshooting Replication Issues**

By the end of this chapter, you will be able to **design, implement, and troubleshoot replication strategies** for SQL Server environments effectively.

1. Overview of SQL Server Replication Types

SQL Server provides different **replication models** depending on the use case, latency requirements, and data consistency needs.

1.1. What is Database Replication?

Replication is the **process of copying and distributing data** from one database (the **Publisher**) to another (the **Subscriber**) in a controlled and automated manner. This ensures that databases across different locations remain **synchronized and up to date**.

✅ **Key Benefits of Replication:**

- **Scalability** – Distributes workloads across multiple servers.

- **High Availability** – Ensures redundancy in case of failures.

- **Data Consistency** – Synchronizes multiple databases in real-time or near real-time.

- **Load Balancing** – Offloads query workloads to secondary databases.

1.2. Types of SQL Server Replication

Replication Type	Best Use Case	How It Works
Transactional Replication	Real-time updates for reporting and analytics	Data changes at the publisher are immediately sent to subscribers
Merge Replication	Offline clients that need bidirectional synchronization	Both publisher and subscriber can update data, and conflicts are resolved
Snapshot Replication	Periodic data refresh for static or rarely changing data	Takes a complete copy of the data and distributes it at scheduled intervals

1.3. Choosing the Right Replication Type

✅ **Use Transactional Replication** when:

- You need **real-time updates** to subscribers.

- You require **low latency** for data changes.

- Subscribers should have **read-only copies** of the data.

✅ **Use Merge Replication** when:

- **Multiple databases** need to make updates independently.

- Clients work **offline** and sync later.

- Data conflicts need **custom resolution rules**.

✅ **Use Snapshot Replication** when:

- **Data rarely changes**, and periodic updates are sufficient.

- You need a **simple, scheduled refresh** of data.

- High transactional consistency is **not required**.

2. Configuring and Managing Transactional Replication

2.1. Understanding Transactional Replication

Transactional Replication is the most commonly used replication method for **real-time data synchronization**. It is well-suited for scenarios where **subscribers require up-to-date read-only copies** of data.

Key Components of Transactional Replication:

- **Publisher** – The source database that **sends** changes.

- **Distributor** – A SQL Server instance that **manages** replication and stores transaction logs.

- **Subscriber** – The database that **receives** changes from the publisher.

✅ **Example Use Case:**

A company has an **OLTP system** where real-time **sales transactions** occur. The business also has a **reporting database** that must always have up-to-date data. Transactional replication is ideal in this scenario.

2.2. Configuring Transactional Replication

Step 1: Enable Replication Features

Before setting up replication, enable the **SQL Server Agent** and ensure the **Replication feature** is installed.

Step 2: Configure the Distributor

1. Open **SQL Server Management Studio (SSMS)**.

2. Navigate to **Replication > Local Publications**.

3. Right-click **Replication** and choose **Configure Distribution**.

4. Select a SQL Server instance as the **Distributor**.

5. Specify a **distribution database** to store replication data.

Step 3: Configure the Publisher

1. Expand **Replication > Local Publications**.

2. Right-click **New Publication** and select the **database to publish**.

3. Choose **Transactional Replication** as the replication type.

4. Select **tables, stored procedures, and views** to replicate.

Step 4: Configure the Subscriber

1. Navigate to **Replication > Local Subscriptions**.

2. Click **New Subscription** and select the **Publisher database**.

3. Choose a **subscription mode**:

   o **Push Subscription** – The publisher pushes data to the subscriber.

   o **Pull Subscription** – The subscriber fetches data from the publisher.

4. Select **Continuous or Scheduled Synchronization**.

2.3. Managing and Monitoring Transactional Replication

Monitor Replication Performance using:

✅ **Replication Monitor** – Tracks errors, latency, and synchronization status.

✅ **Performance Counters** – Use SQLServer:Replication Agents to monitor agent activity.

✅ **Dynamic Management Views (DMVs)** –

sql

```
SELECT * FROM msdb.dbo.MSdistribution_history;
```

Common Maintenance Tasks:

- Regularly check the **Replication Agent jobs** in SQL Server Agent.

- Clean up **old transactions** from the distribution database using:

sql

```
EXEC sp_MSdistribution_cleanup @min_distretention = 0, @max_distretention = 72;
```

- Monitor **latency issues** and adjust **batch sizes** for better performance.

3. Data Synchronization Techniques for Distributed Databases

3.1. Importance of Data Synchronization

In distributed environments, keeping databases synchronized ensures **data consistency, redundancy, and operational efficiency**. The key challenges in data synchronization include:

✓ **Latency Reduction** – Ensuring data changes propagate quickly.

✓ **Conflict Resolution** – Handling cases where multiple sources update the same data.

✓ **Scalability** – Managing large volumes of replicated data efficiently.

3.2. Techniques for Data Synchronization

1. Change Data Capture (CDC):

- Tracks changes in a database **without using triggers**.

- Captures inserts, updates, and deletes **efficiently**.

- Use case: Synchronizing SQL Server with **data warehouses**.

sql

```
EXEC sys.sp_cdc_enable_table @source_schema = 'dbo',
@source_name = 'Orders', @role_name = NULL;
```

2. Change Tracking:

- Provides a **lightweight** alternative to CDC.

- Tracks changes **without storing historical data**.

- Useful for mobile applications that require **offline data sync**.

sql

```
ALTER        DATABASE        MyDatabase        SET
CHANGE_TRACKING = ON;
```

3. Bi-Directional Replication (Merge Replication):

- Synchronizes changes **in both directions** between two databases.

- Requires conflict resolution logic.

✅ **Best Practice:** Use **Merge Replication** only when **bi-directional synchronization is necessary,** as it **introduces performance overhead**.

4. Troubleshooting Replication Issues

4.1. Common Replication Problems and Fixes

Issue	Possible Cause	Solution
Latency issues	High transaction load	Increase batch size or use pull subscriptions
Subscription failure	Network issues or incorrect settings	Check subscriber connectivity and firewall settings

Replication Agent fails	Permissions issue	Ensure SQL Agent has necessary permissions
Data conflicts	Bi-directional replication	Configure conflict resolution rules

4.2. Debugging Replication Failures

✅ **Check Error Logs**

sql

SELECT * FROM msdb.dbo.MSdistribution_history ORDER BY time DESC;

✅ **Verify Replication Agents**

Use **Replication Monitor** to check agent status:

sql

EXEC sp_replmonitorhelppublication;

✅ **Reinitialize Subscriptions**

If replication is stuck, **force a re-sync:**

sql

```sql
EXEC sp_reinitmergepullsubscription @publisher = 'MyPublisher', @publication = 'MyPublication
```

PART 5: SCALABILITY, BUSINESS INTELLIGENCE, AND FUTURE TRENDS

Chapter 14: Scaling SQL Server for Enterprise Workloads

As businesses grow and data volumes increase, **scalability** becomes a crucial factor in database performance and reliability. SQL Server, widely used in enterprise environments, must handle **large-scale workloads, high transaction volumes, and multi-tenant architectures** while maintaining performance and availability.

Scaling SQL Server effectively requires a **strategic approach** that balances hardware capabilities, database design, and efficient query processing. This chapter explores **key scaling strategies** and their implementation in **enterprise workloads**, covering:

- **Horizontal vs. Vertical Scaling Strategies**

- **Partitioning, Sharding, and Distributed Databases**

- **Load Balancing and Performance Considerations**

- **SQL Server in Multi-Tenant Architectures**

By the end of this chapter, you will understand **how to scale SQL Server for performance, reliability, and cost efficiency** while ensuring **optimal data distribution and query execution**.

1. Horizontal vs. Vertical Scaling Strategies

1.1. Understanding Scaling in SQL Server

Scaling refers to increasing a database system's capacity to handle **growing workloads** efficiently. There are two primary approaches to scaling SQL Server:

- **Vertical Scaling (Scaling Up)** – Adding more **CPU, RAM, and storage** to a single database server.

- **Horizontal Scaling (Scaling Out)** – Distributing data across **multiple servers** to share the workload.

✅ **Key Considerations When Scaling:**

- **Transaction throughput** – Can the database handle **millions of transactions per second (TPS)?**

- **Query performance** – How quickly can SQL Server **process complex queries**?

- **Fault tolerance** – Can the system handle **failures** without downtime?

1.2. Vertical Scaling (Scaling Up)

Vertical scaling increases SQL Server's capacity by **upgrading hardware resources** on a single machine.

✅ **Common Upgrades in Vertical Scaling:**

Component	Upgrade Option	Impact
CPU	Add more cores or switch to a faster processor	Increases query execution speed
RAM	Expand memory from 64GB to 256GB+	Reduces disk I/O and increases cache efficiency
Storage	Upgrade to SSDs or NVMe drives	Improves read/write performance
Network	10Gbps+ NICs	Reduces latency for high-volume data transfers

Best for: OLTP workloads where a single **high-performance database server** can meet demands.

1.3. Horizontal Scaling (Scaling Out)

Horizontal **scaling** involves **distributing database workloads across multiple servers**, allowing for better scalability and fault tolerance.

✅ **Techniques for Horizontal Scaling:**

Technique	How It Works	Use Case
Database Replication	Copies data across multiple servers for read scalability	Reporting, analytics
Sharding	Splits a database into smaller chunks, distributed across multiple servers	Large-scale applications
Federation	Divides database tables into separate, independent databases	Multi-tenant architectures

Best for: Enterprise systems, high-volume transactions, and cloud-based applications that require dynamic scaling.

2. Partitioning, Sharding, and Distributed Databases

2.1. Database Partitioning

Partitioning splits large tables into **smaller, more manageable segments** for improved performance.

Types of Partitioning:

Partitioning Type	Description	Use Case
Range Partitioning	Splits data based on a **range of values** (e.g., orders by year)	Time-series data, logs
List Partitioning	Divides data based on a **specific column value** (e.g., region)	Multi-country applications
Hash Partitioning	Uses a **hash function** to distribute data evenly	Load balancing in high-volume databases

Example: Creating a Range Partitioned Table in SQL Server

sql

```sql
CREATE PARTITION FUNCTION OrderDateRange (DATETIME)
AS RANGE LEFT FOR VALUES ('2021-01-01', '2022-01-01', '2023-01-01');


CREATE PARTITION SCHEME OrderScheme
AS PARTITION OrderDateRange
ALL TO ([PRIMARY]);


CREATE TABLE Orders
(
    OrderID INT PRIMARY KEY,
    OrderDate DATETIME
) ON OrderScheme(OrderDate);
```

✅ **Benefits of Partitioning:**

- **Speeds up query performance** by reducing the amount of scanned data.

- **Improves backup and maintenance efficiency** by allowing partial backups.

2.2. Sharding: Distributing Data Across Multiple Servers

Sharding splits large databases into **multiple independent databases** called **shards**, where each shard **stores a subset of the data**.

✅ **Sharding Strategies:**

- **Key-Based Sharding** – Data is distributed based on a specific column (e.g., CustomerID MOD 4).

- **Geo-Based Sharding** – Data is split based on geography (e.g., Europe vs. North America).

- **Range-Based Sharding** – Data is divided based on a numeric range (e.g., UserID 1-1000 in one shard, 1001-2000 in another).

🚀 **Best for: High-scale applications like e-commerce platforms and SaaS applications.**

Example: Assigning Customers to Shards

sql

```sql
IF (CustomerID % 4 = 0)
    INSERT INTO Shard1.Customers VALUES (@CustomerID, @Name);
ELSE IF (CustomerID % 4 = 1)
    INSERT INTO Shard2.Customers VALUES (@CustomerID, @Name);
```

✅ **Benefits of Sharding:**

- **Eliminates single-server bottlenecks.**

- **Allows databases to scale horizontally.**

3. Load Balancing and Performance Considerations

3.1. Load Balancing in SQL Server

Load balancing **distributes database requests** across multiple servers to **avoid overload and improve response times.**

✅ **Load Balancing Strategies:**

Strategy	Description	Use Case
Read-Only Replicas	Offloads read queries to secondary servers	Reporting, analytics
Database Connection Pooling	Reuses existing database connections to reduce latency	Web applications, APIs
Application-Level Load Balancing	Distributes queries across multiple database instances	High-traffic SaaS applications

🏴 **Best for:** Applications experiencing **high concurrent database requests.**

3.2. Performance Optimization in Large Workloads

Techniques to Improve Performance in Large-Scale SQL Server Workloads:

✅ **Use Indexing**

- Optimize **clustered and non-clustered indexes** to reduce query execution times.

✅ **Optimize Query Execution Plans**

- Analyze execution plans to **eliminate table scans and optimize joins**.

✅ **Use Caching Mechanisms**

- Implement **query caching** using **Redis** or **in-memory OLTP**.

✅ **Optimize TempDB Configuration**

- Use multiple **TempDB files** to **avoid contention**:

sql

```
ALTER DATABASE tempdb ADD FILE (NAME =
tempdev2, FILENAME = 'D:\tempdb2.mdf', SIZE = 1GB,
FILEGROWTH = 512MB);
```

4. SQL Server in Multi-Tenant Architectures

4.1. Understanding Multi-Tenant Architectures

In multi-tenant environments, a **single SQL Server instance**
serves **multiple customers (tenants)**. There are three primary
approaches:

Architecture Type	Description	Use Case
Shared Database, Shared Schema	All tenants use **one database and one schema**	Small SaaS applications
Shared Database, Separate Schemas	Each tenant has its **own schema** but shares the database	Mid-sized SaaS platforms

Separate Databases per Tenant	Each tenant has **its own database**	Large-scale, enterprise SaaS

🚀 **Best for: Cloud SaaS applications requiring tenant isolation and scalability.**

✓ **Security Considerations in Multi-Tenant Databases:**

- Use **Row-Level Security (RLS)** to restrict access by tenant:

sql

CREATE SECURITY POLICY TenantSecurityPolicy

ADD FILTER PREDICATE TenantFilter(TenantID) ON dbo.Customers;

- Encrypt tenant data using **Always Encrypted**.

Chapter 15: SQL Server and Business Intelligence (BI) Integration

In today's data-driven world, businesses need **real-time insights** to make informed decisions. **Business Intelligence (BI)** helps transform raw data into meaningful information through **reporting, analytics, and data visualization**. SQL Server provides a robust ecosystem of BI tools, including:

- **SQL Server Reporting Services (SSRS)** for creating and managing reports.

- **SQL Server Analysis Services (SSAS)** for data warehousing and analytics.

- **SQL Server Integration Services (SSIS)** for Extract, Transform, Load (**ETL**) processes.

- **Power BI** for interactive data visualization and dashboards.

This chapter explores how SQL Server integrates with these BI tools to deliver **scalable, high-performance business intelligence solutions**.

1. Introduction to SQL Server Reporting Services (SSRS)

1.1. What is SQL Server Reporting Services (SSRS)?

SQL Server Reporting Services (SSRS) is a **reporting and data visualization tool** that allows businesses to create, manage, and distribute reports based on SQL Server data.

✅ **Key Features of SSRS:**

- **Tabular and graphical reports** – Supports **tables, charts, maps, and KPIs**.

- **Parameter-based reports** – Users can filter data dynamically.

- **Subscription-based report delivery** – Automates report distribution via email or file shares.

- **Integration with Power BI** – SSRS can be used alongside Power BI for enhanced reporting.

🚀 Best for: Enterprise reporting, operational dashboards, and scheduled report distribution.

1.2. SSRS Architecture

Component	Description
Report Server	Hosts and processes reports.
Report Manager	Web-based portal to view and manage reports.
Report Builder	A tool to create and edit reports.
Data Sources	SQL Server, Excel, Oracle, and other databases.

1.3. Creating a Simple SSRS Report

Step 1: Install and Configure SSRS

1. Download **SQL Server Reporting Services (SSRS)** from Microsoft.

2. Install SSRS and configure the **Report Server**.

3. Open **SQL Server Management Studio (SSMS)** and connect to the **Report Server instance**.

Step 2: Create a New SSRS Report

1. Open **Report Builder** or Visual Studio with the SSRS template.

2. Choose a **data source (SQL Server, Oracle, etc.)**.

3. Create a **dataset** using a T-SQL query:

sql

```
SELECT CustomerID, Name, SalesAmount FROM SalesData
WHERE Year = 2024;
```

4. Drag a **Table, Chart, or KPI component** onto the report canvas.

5. Save and deploy the report to the **Report Server**.

Step 3: Schedule Automated Report Delivery

- Configure a **Subscription** to send reports via **email or shared folder**.

✅ **Best Practice**: Use **SSRS caching and snapshots** to optimize performance for large reports.

2. SQL Server Analysis Services (SSAS) for Data Warehousing

2.1. What is SSAS?

SQL Server Analysis Services (SSAS) is a **data modeling and analytics** tool that enables businesses to build **data warehouses, multidimensional cubes, and tabular models** for BI applications.

✅ **Key Features of SSAS:**

- **OLAP (Online Analytical Processing)** – Enables **fast query performance** on large datasets.

- **Data Cubes** – Store pre-aggregated data for rapid analysis.

- **Tabular Models** – Simplifies reporting with in-memory data storage.

- **Role-based security** – Controls access to data at the row level.

Best for: Enterprise-scale data warehousing, predictive analytics, and KPI tracking.

2.2. SSAS Architecture

Component	Description
Data Source	SQL Server, Azure SQL, or other databases.
Data Model	Stores dimensions, measures, and hierarchies.
Processing Engine	Aggregates and stores data for analysis.
Client Tools	Excel, Power BI, SSMS, and custom BI applications.

2.3. Building an SSAS Cube for Data Analysis

Step 1: Create an SSAS Project in Visual Studio

1. Open **SQL Server Data Tools (SSDT)**.

2. Create a **New Analysis Services Project**.

3. Select **Multidimensional and Data Mining Model**.

Step 2: Define a Data Source and Cube Structure

1. Connect to the SQL Server **Data Warehouse**.

2. Define **Measures** (e.g., Total Sales, Profit Margin).

3. Define **Dimensions** (e.g., Customers, Products, Regions).

Step 3: Process and Deploy the Cube

1. Click **Process** to aggregate and store data.

2. Deploy the cube to **SSAS Server**.

3. Use **Excel or Power BI** to analyze the cube.

✅ **Best Practice**: Use **Partitioning and Aggregations** to optimize query performance.

3. Extract, Transform, Load (ETL) with SQL Server Integration Services (SSIS)

3.1. What is SSIS?

SQL Server Integration Services (SSIS) is a **data integration and ETL (Extract, Transform, Load) tool** that allows businesses to move and transform data between systems.

✅ **Key Features of SSIS:**

- **Data extraction** from SQL Server, Oracle, MySQL, and APIs.

- **Data transformation** (cleansing, deduplication, aggregation).

- **Data loading** into data warehouses and operational databases.

- **Automated workflows** for ETL processing.

🚀 **Best for: Enterprise ETL pipelines, cloud data migration, and data warehouse integration.**

3.2. Building an SSIS ETL Package

Step 1: Create an SSIS Project in Visual Studio

1. Open **SQL Server Data Tools (SSDT)**.

2. Select **Integration Services Project**.

Step 2: Configure ETL Workflow

1. **Extract Data** from a SQL Server database using an **OLE DB Source**.

2. **Transform Data** using a **Data Flow Task** (e.g., remove duplicates, format dates).

3. **Load Data** into the data warehouse using an **OLE DB Destination**.

Step 3: Automate ETL Process with SQL Server Agent

1. Deploy the **SSIS Package** to SQL Server.

2. Create a **SQL Server Agent Job** to schedule the ETL process.

✅ **Best Practice**: Use **SSIS logging and error handling** to track failed data loads.

4. Power BI Integration for Data Visualization

4.1. What is Power BI?

Power BI is a cloud-based **data visualization and analytics tool** that connects to SQL Server and SSAS for **interactive dashboards and reports**.

✓ **Key Features of Power BI:**

- **Live dashboards** for real-time analytics.

- **Data connectivity** with SQL Server, SSAS, and cloud data sources.

- **DAX (Data Analysis Expressions)** for advanced calculations.

- **AI-powered insights** to detect trends and anomalies.

🚀 **Best for: Self-service BI, executive dashboards, and interactive reporting.**

4.2. Connecting Power BI to SQL Server

Step 1: Import SQL Server Data

1. Open **Power BI Desktop**.

2. Click **Get Data > SQL Server**.

3. Enter the **server name** and database credentials.

Step 2: Create Data Models and Visualizations

1. Select **Tables and Views** from SQL Server.

2. Create **Measures and Calculated Columns** using DAX.

3. Build **Dashboards with Charts, Tables, and KPIs**.

Step 3: Publish Reports to Power BI Service

1. Click **Publish** to upload reports to **Power BI Cloud**.

2. Set up **Scheduled Data Refresh**.

3. Share reports with stakeholders.

✅ **Best Practice**: Use **DirectQuery mode** for real-time SQL Server analytics.

Chapter 16: SQL Server and AI-Driven Performance Optimization

As the demands on database performance continue to grow, **artificial intelligence (AI)** and **machine learning (ML)** are increasingly being integrated into SQL Server environments to optimize query performance, monitor system health, and predict future workloads. SQL Server's advanced capabilities, such as **Machine Learning Services** and **AI-powered anomaly detection**, enable database administrators (DBAs) and developers to leverage these technologies for smarter, more efficient database management.

This chapter explores how **AI and machine learning** can be applied to **optimize database performance**. We will cover the following topics:

- **Machine Learning Services in SQL Server**

- **AI-Based Anomaly Detection for Performance Monitoring**

- **Automating Query Optimization with AI and Machine Learning**

- **Predictive Analytics for Database Performance**

By the end of this chapter, you will have a deep understanding of how to leverage **AI-driven tools** to enhance performance, **automate optimization tasks,** and **anticipate future database needs**.

1. Machine Learning Services in SQL Server

1.1. Introduction to Machine Learning in SQL Server

SQL Server Machine Learning Services (formerly SQL Server R Services) integrates **advanced analytics** into SQL Server, allowing you to run machine learning models directly within the database. This service supports languages such as **R** and **Python**, enabling users to create and execute **AI models** and perform **predictive analytics** on the data without needing to move it outside of the SQL Server environment.

Key Components of Machine Learning Services:

- **In-database execution**: Allows machine learning models to run **directly within the database**, which eliminates the need for data extraction and minimizes data movement.

- **Support for R and Python**: You can use **Python libraries** like **TensorFlow, Keras**, or **scikit-learn** for model training, as well as **R** packages for statistical analysis.

- **Data Preparation and Analysis**: SQL Server provides tools to **cleanse, transform**, and **prepare data** for machine learning processes, making it easier to build models using the data within the SQL Server instance.

1.2. Setting Up Machine Learning Services in SQL Server

To use Machine Learning Services in SQL Server, you need to install the **R** and/or **Python** integration during SQL Server installation.

Steps to Enable Python and R in SQL Server:

1. During SQL Server installation, select the **Machine Learning Services** option.

2. Choose **Python** and/or **R** depending on your requirements.

3. After installation, configure SQL Server to enable the execution of external scripts:

sql

Copy

```
sp_configure 'external scripts enabled', 1;

RECONFIGURE;
```

4. Verify the installation by running an example R or Python script inside SQL Server:

sql

Copy

```
EXEC sp_execute_external_script
    @language = N'R',
    @script = N'outputDataSet <- data.frame("Message" = "Hello, SQL Server!")',
    @output_data_1_name = N'outputDataSet';
```

1.3. Machine Learning Use Cases in SQL Server

Machine Learning Services can be applied in many areas for performance optimization:

- **Predictive Maintenance**: Detect patterns in **server performance metrics** to predict hardware failures or issues that could affect database performance.

- **Anomaly Detection**: Identify outliers and **suspicious behavior** in query performance, such as spikes in query execution time or high resource consumption.

- **Query Performance Prediction**: Use historical query performance data to **predict future resource usage** and optimize query execution plans.

2. AI-Based Anomaly Detection for Performance Monitoring

2.1. Understanding AI-Based Anomaly Detection

Anomaly detection in SQL Server uses **machine learning algorithms** to identify unusual patterns in **performance metrics**, such as **CPU usage**, **query execution times**, **memory usage**, and **disk I/O**. By leveraging AI, we can detect performance issues before they become critical.

AI models analyze historical **performance data** and establish **baseline behavior** for SQL Server operations. Any deviation from this baseline, such as unexpected spikes or drops, is flagged as an anomaly.

Common Anomalies in SQL Server Performance:

- **High CPU usage**: Continuous high CPU usage can indicate inefficient queries, missing indexes, or hardware failures.

- **Slow Query Performance**: A sudden increase in query execution times could signal suboptimal query plans, database locking, or missing resources.

- **Memory Leaks**: An increase in memory usage over time might indicate issues such as **poorly optimized queries** or **poor memory management**.

2.2. Implementing Anomaly Detection Using Machine Learning

SQL Server allows you to implement **AI-based anomaly detection models** directly within the database. For example, you can create a **predictive model** that flags queries with abnormal execution times or system resource usage.

Example: Using Python for Anomaly Detection in SQL Server

Here is how you might implement a simple **anomaly detection model** using Python's **scikit-learn** in SQL Server:

1. **Gather Historical Data**: Collect performance data, such as **CPU usage** and **query execution times** over a period.

sql

Copy

```sql
SELECT
    CPUUsage,
    QueryDuration
FROM PerformanceMetrics;
```

2. **Train the Model**: Use the data to train an **Isolation Forest model** in Python that can detect outliers.

python

Copy

```python
from sklearn.ensemble import IsolationForest
import pandas as pd


# Load performance data into a pandas DataFrame
```

```python
data = pd.read_sql("SELECT CPUUsage, QueryDuration FROM PerformanceMetrics", conn)


# Train Isolation Forest model
model = IsolationForest(contamination=0.05)  # 5% outliers expected
model.fit(data)
predictions = model.predict(data)


# Identify outliers (anomalies)
anomalies = data[predictions == -1]
```

3. **Deploy the Model**: After training, deploy the model to SQL Server and use it for real-time anomaly detection.

sql

Copy

```sql
EXEC sp_execute_external_script
    @language = N'Python',
```

```sql
@script = N'from sklearn.ensemble import IsolationForest;
model = IsolationForest(); model.fit(data)',

@input_data_1_name = N'data',

@output_data_1_name = N'anomalies';
```

2.3. Automating Anomaly Detection Alerts

Once anomalies are detected, SQL Server can trigger alerts through **SQL Server Agent** to notify administrators of performance issues:

1. **Create an Alert**:

   o Set up an alert in **SQL Server Agent** to send **email notifications** when certain anomalies (e.g., high CPU usage) are detected.

sql

Copy

```sql
EXEC msdb.dbo.sp_add_alert
    @name = N'High CPU Usage',
    @message_id = 50000,
    @severity = 16,
```

```
@notification_message = N'Anomaly detected: CPU usage
exceeds threshold.';
```

2. **Integrate with Power BI**: Visualize detected
   anomalies in **Power BI** for real-time monitoring
   dashboards.

3. Automating Query Optimization with AI and Machine Learning

3.1. AI and Machine Learning for Query Performance Tuning

Machine learning can assist in **automating query optimization** by analyzing historical query performance data and **predicting which indexes, execution plans, and query patterns** will optimize future queries.

AI-Driven Query Optimization Example:

1. **Data Collection**: Collect historical performance
   metrics, including query execution times, execution
   plans, and resource usage.

2. **Model Training**: Train a machine learning model using algorithms such as **Random Forest, Gradient Boosting,** or **Neural Networks** to predict query execution times based on the available features (e.g., query structure, table size, indexing strategy).

3. **Prediction and Optimization**: Use the model's predictions to suggest optimal **indexes** and **query execution plans**.

Example:

The model identifies that a specific query would benefit from an additional **non-clustered index** on a frequently queried column. SQL Server can then **automatically suggest or apply** this index to improve future query performance.

3.2. Using AI to Automatically Generate Indexes

An example of using machine learning for **index optimization** might involve training a model to analyze query execution plans and recommend missing or underutilized indexes based on historical query performance.

- **Query Execution History**: Gather data on queries with long execution times or frequent table scans.

- **Train the Model**: The model identifies patterns in the queries that suggest **missing indexes** or inefficient joins.

- **Create and Apply Recommendations**: Based on the model's output, SQL Server automatically creates the suggested indexes or notifies the DBA for manual review.

4. Predictive Analytics for Database Performance

4.1. Predictive Analytics Overview

Predictive analytics uses historical data and machine learning models to **forecast future system performance**. In the context of SQL Server, predictive analytics can help **anticipate database workload spikes, resource utilization, and potential failures**.

Common Use Cases for Predictive Analytics in SQL Server:

- **Predicting Query Load**: Analyzing historical query patterns to predict future query traffic, allowing the DBA to scale resources accordingly.

- **Forecasting Disk Space Usage**: Predicting when disk space will run out based on historical data and setting up automated alerts before the issue occurs.

- **Forecasting CPU and Memory Usage**: Anticipating resource demands during high-traffic periods, such as seasonal spikes in website traffic or end-of-quarter reporting.

4.2. Building a Predictive Model for SQL Server Performance

Step 1: Collect Historical Data

Collect **CPU usage, query execution times**, and **I/O stats** over a period of weeks or months. This data is used to **train the predictive model**.

Step 2: Train the Predictive Model

Using Python's **scikit-learn** or **TensorFlow**, train a model to predict system performance:

python

Copy

```python
import pandas as pd

from sklearn.ensemble import RandomForestRegressor


# Load performance data
data = pd.read_sql("SELECT CPUUsage, QueryDuration, MemoryUsage FROM ServerMetrics", conn)


# Prepare features and target variable
X = data[['CPUUsage', 'MemoryUsage']]

y = data['QueryDuration']


# Train the model
model = RandomForestRegressor()

model.fit(X, y)
```

```
# Predict query duration based on future CPU and memory usage

predictions = model.predict(X_new)
```

Step 3: Apply Predictions to Performance Management

Use the predicted performance metrics to set thresholds, **automatically adjust resource allocation**, or trigger preventive maintenance tasks.

Chapter 17: Future Trends in SQL Server Administration

The role of a **SQL Server Database Administrator (DBA)** is evolving rapidly in response to technological advancements. With the rise of cloud computing, machine learning, artificial intelligence (AI), and the increasing demand for **real-time analytics**, the future of SQL Server administration looks very different from its past. SQL Server has already seen major changes in recent years, but there are even more significant advancements on the horizon, especially with the upcoming release of **SQL Server 2025**.

In this chapter, we will explore:

- **SQL Server 2025 and Beyond: What's Next?**

- **Evolution of Database Administration in a Cloud-First World**

- **NoSQL vs. SQL: The Future of Relational Databases**

- **Career Growth and Certifications for SQL Server Professionals**

By the end of this chapter, you will have insights into **the future of SQL Server** and **how database administrators can evolve their skills** to stay competitive in an ever-changing technological landscape.

1. SQL Server 2025 and Beyond: What's Next?

1.1. Anticipating Features in SQL Server 2025

As we look towards **SQL Server 2025**, Microsoft continues to improve the platform to meet the growing needs of businesses in areas such as **performance, scalability, security**, and **cloud integration**. SQL Server 2025 will likely introduce several new features that will shape the future of **enterprise database management**. Some of the anticipated features include:

1.1.1. Enhanced Cloud Integration

The trend of **cloud-first** database management is likely to continue with SQL Server 2025, which will introduce **more seamless integration with Microsoft Azure** and other cloud platforms. SQL Server will increasingly operate in **hybrid environments**, enabling **on-premises databases** to easily connect with cloud services for storage, processing, and backup.

Features Likely to Be Included:

- **Automated cloud backups and disaster recovery.**

- **Enhanced hybrid cloud data management tools.**

- **Cloud-native performance tuning and scaling features.**

1.1.2. AI-Powered Performance Optimization

SQL Server 2025 is expected to take advantage of **machine learning and AI** to automatically optimize **query performance, indexing, and resource allocation**. Future versions will likely include more **AI-driven features** that automatically adjust to **workload changes** and **predict future resource requirements**, making SQL Server more adaptive to varying conditions.

Potential New Features:

- **Automated index management** using AI to analyze and rebuild indexes.

- **Machine learning models** for query optimization based on historical data.

1.1.3. Advanced Security Features

As **data security** becomes increasingly important, SQL Server 2025 will likely include **enhanced encryption technologies** and **security features** designed to protect data from cyber threats. **End-to-end encryption, data masking**, and **identity**

management will become more sophisticated and integrated into the SQL Server ecosystem.

Anticipated Features:

- **Data encryption with machine learning-based threat detection.**

- **Stronger integration with Azure Active Directory** for identity and access management.

- **Advanced auditing** capabilities and **compliance features** to meet new privacy regulations.

1.1.4. Increased Focus on Real-Time Analytics

With the rise of **real-time business intelligence (BI)**, SQL Server 2025 will likely improve the way it handles **real-time data ingestion** and **analytics**. Integration with **streaming data sources** and **edge computing** will become more robust, enabling organizations to perform **analytics on live data** as it is generated.

Expected Features:

- **Real-time analytics processing** on **high-velocity data streams.**

- **Seamless integration with Power BI** for live reporting and dashboards.

1.2. Future of SQL Server in a Hybrid Cloud World

The future of SQL Server is undoubtedly cloud-centric, and SQL Server 2025 will focus heavily on providing a seamless experience for businesses operating in hybrid cloud environments. **SQL Server in Azure** will be deeply integrated with **Azure Synapse Analytics, Azure Machine Learning**, and **Azure Data Lake**, providing **unified analytics** across on-premises and cloud databases.

Hybrid Cloud Features Likely to Be Introduced:

- **Azure Arc-enabled SQL Server**: SQL Server will likely support more advanced hybrid cloud features with **Azure Arc**, allowing users to manage both on-prem and cloud-based SQL Servers from a single interface.

- **SQL Server in Containers**: The ability to run SQL Server on **containers** (e.g., Kubernetes) will make it easier to deploy and scale SQL Server across hybrid and multi-cloud environments.

2. Evolution of Database Administration in a Cloud-First World

2.1. The Shift Toward Cloud-First Architecture

In the past, database administration was mostly focused on managing **on-premises infrastructure** and ensuring that systems remained reliable. However, with the advent of cloud technologies, the role of **DBAs** is shifting towards managing **cloud-based databases** and integrating them into a broader IT ecosystem.

The cloud-first architecture encourages businesses to **migrate to the cloud** for **scalability, flexibility**, and **cost efficiency**. As more organizations adopt **hybrid cloud and multi-cloud environments**, SQL Server DBAs must adapt to **cloud-native deployment strategies**.

Key Changes for DBAs in Cloud-First Architecture:

- **Focus on cloud management tools** such as **Azure SQL Database, AWS RDS**, and **Google Cloud SQL**.

- **Increased automation** in database administration tasks like backups, performance tuning, and scaling.

- **Emphasis on security** in cloud environments, including **identity management, encryption**, and **compliance**.

2.2. Automation and AI in Database Administration

With the increasing complexity of managing databases, automation and AI are becoming integral parts of the **SQL Server DBA role**. In the cloud-first world, DBAs will rely on **machine learning** to **automate** tasks such as:

- **Query optimization**

- **Index management**

- **Data consistency checks**

- **Resource scaling**

AI-powered tools will **monitor database health, identify issues** before they become critical, and **recommend**

corrective actions automatically, reducing the workload for DBAs.

Automation Tools to Expect:

- **Self-healing databases** powered by **machine learning** algorithms.

- **Automated patching and updates** without downtime.

- **AI-based performance tuning** that adjusts queries and indexing based on workload patterns.

3. NoSQL vs. SQL: The Future of Relational Databases

3.1. The Rise of NoSQL Databases

As businesses increasingly rely on **unstructured data** (such as social media, logs, and IoT data), **NoSQL** databases have gained traction as an alternative to traditional **relational databases**. **NoSQL** databases, such as **MongoDB**, **Cassandra**, and **Couchbase**, are designed to handle massive volumes of **unstructured data** and are often more scalable than traditional **SQL databases**.

Benefits of NoSQL:

- **Scalability**: NoSQL databases are often designed for **horizontal scaling,** allowing them to handle massive datasets without compromising performance.

- **Flexibility**: NoSQL databases are schema-less, enabling faster changes and more flexibility in how data is stored.

Challenges of NoSQL:

- **Consistency**: NoSQL databases use **eventual consistency** rather than strict consistency, which might not be suitable for transactional systems.

- **Limited Analytical Capabilities**: NoSQL databases are less suited for complex **analytical queries** and **reporting**.

3.2. SQL vs. NoSQL: Where Do They Fit in the Future?

Despite the rise of NoSQL databases, **SQL databases** remain crucial for **transactional systems, business intelligence**, and **data consistency**. SQL Server's future will likely involve **hybrid architectures** that combine the strengths of both SQL and NoSQL technologies.

Where SQL and NoSQL Will Coexist:

- **SQL for transactional applications** (e.g., financial transactions, inventory management) where **ACID compliance** and **data consistency** are essential.

- **NoSQL for big data and unstructured data** (e.g., social media feeds, sensor data) where **schema flexibility** and **horizontal scaling** are more important.

3.3. SQL Server's Role in the NoSQL Era

As SQL Server evolves, **integration with NoSQL systems** like **MongoDB** will allow DBAs to build hybrid databases that can handle both **structured** and **unstructured data**. SQL Server 2025 and beyond may offer enhanced **NoSQL integration** capabilities, enabling users to perform analytics across **relational and non-relational data**.

4. Career Growth and Certifications for SQL Server Professionals

4.1. The Evolving Role of SQL Server DBAs

As the landscape of database administration changes, SQL Server professionals must continuously evolve their skills. The **cloud-first** world, the **adoption of machine learning**, and the rise of **NoSQL databases** are driving significant changes in the role of the **SQL Server DBA**.

Skills Required for the Future DBA:

- **Cloud Technologies**: Proficiency in **Azure, AWS**, and **Google Cloud** for managing cloud-based SQL Server instances.

- **Automation**: Knowledge of tools like **Azure Automation, PowerShell**, and **Ansible** for automating tasks.

- **AI and Machine Learning**: Understanding how to leverage **AI-powered performance tuning, predictive analytics**, and **data optimization**.

- **NoSQL Databases**: Familiarity with integrating **SQL Server with NoSQL databases** for hybrid data environments.

4.2. Certifications for SQL Server Professionals

Certifications are crucial for staying current in the rapidly evolving database landscape. The following certifications will be valuable for SQL Server professionals in the coming years:

1. **Microsoft Certified: Azure Database Administrator Associate**

   o Covers **Azure SQL Database, SQL Server on Azure VMs**, and **hybrid environments**.

2. **Microsoft Certified: Data Analyst Associate**

   o Focuses on **Power BI, data visualization**, and **analytics** with SQL Server.

3. **Microsoft Certified: Azure Solutions Architect Expert**

   o Involves designing cloud solutions using **Azure SQL** and other Microsoft data tools.

4. Certified Kubernetes Administrator (CKA)

- o SQL Server DBAs working with **Kubernetes** for containerized SQL Server instances should consider this certification.

Appendices & Resources

Appendix A: SQL Server Best Practices Checklist

Ensuring that SQL Server is configured correctly and maintained properly is essential for maximizing performance, security, and availability. This checklist provides a comprehensive set of **best practices** for SQL Server administrators to follow for optimal configuration, performance tuning, and maintenance.

1. SQL Server Installation and Configuration

- **SQL Server Edition Selection:**
    - Choose the appropriate **SQL Server edition** (Standard, Enterprise, or Web) based on **business requirements, workload size**, and **budget**.
    - Ensure that the edition supports the required **features** (e.g., **Always On Availability Groups, SQL Server Agent, Data Warehousing**).

- **Instance Configuration**:

  - Configure **SQL Server instance** according to best practices for **security** and **performance**.

  - Use a **service account** with the **least privileges** necessary for SQL Server services (e.g., SQL Server Agent, Database Engine).

  - Assign a **named instance** if you are installing multiple instances on the same server to avoid conflicts.

- **TempDB Configuration**:

  - Allocate **multiple data files** for **TempDB** (equal size to avoid contention). Typically, **1 data file per processor core** is recommended.

  - Ensure **TempDB** is placed on a **fast disk** (preferably SSD) to optimize performance.

  - Set **TempDB's autogrowth** to a fixed size (e.g., 1GB) to avoid excessive autogrowth events during peak usage.

2. Database Design and Architecture

- **Normalization**:

  o Ensure **database normalization** to minimize data redundancy and maintain data integrity.

  o Use **denormalization** cautiously for specific reporting requirements where performance is critical.

- **Indexing**:

  o **Regularly monitor index fragmentation** and rebuild or reorganize indexes based on fragmentation level (usually above 30%).

  o Use **clustered indexes** on columns frequently used for searching or sorting.

  o Create **non-clustered indexes** on columns used in **WHERE** clauses, **JOINs**, and **ORDER BY**.

  o **Avoid excessive indexes**; create only those necessary for improving query performance.

- **Data Types**:

- Choose appropriate **data types** based on column usage (e.g., use **INT** for integer values and **DATETIME** for date/time fields).

- Avoid **using VARCHAR(MAX)** unless absolutely necessary to reduce overhead.

3. Performance Tuning

- **Query Optimization**:

  - Ensure queries are **written efficiently** by using appropriate **JOINs** (avoid Cartesian products) and **WHERE** clauses.

  - Use **EXPLAIN plans** to analyze the **query execution plan** and **optimize slow-running queries**.

  - *Avoid SELECT ;* always specify only the necessary columns.

  - Use **indexed views** for complex aggregations and summarization tasks.

- **Resource Allocation**:

- Set appropriate values for **max server memory** to avoid **memory starvation** and **ensure sufficient memory** for the operating system and other processes.

- Configure **maximum degree of parallelism (MAXDOP)** to avoid excessive parallelism and improve query performance, especially for OLTP systems.

- Regularly **monitor CPU, memory, and disk I/O** usage using **Performance Monitor** or **SQL Server Management Studio (SSMS)**.

- **SQL Server Agent Jobs**:

  - Regularly monitor and schedule **database maintenance tasks** such as backups, index rebuilds, and integrity checks using **SQL Server Agent jobs**.

  - Configure **alerts** for critical events like job failures, database growth thresholds, and deadlocks.

4. Backup and Recovery

- **Backup Strategy**:

  - Implement a **backup strategy** that includes **full, differential**, and **transaction log backups**.

  - Schedule **regular backups** and store backups in multiple locations (on-premises and off-site).

  - **Test restore procedures** regularly to ensure that backups can be successfully restored when needed.

- **Backup Retention**:

  - Ensure **backup retention** policies align with **business requirements** and regulatory compliance (e.g., PCI-DSS, HIPAA).

  - Set up **automated backups** with **SQL Server Agent jobs** for daily, weekly, and monthly backups.

5. High Availability and Disaster Recovery

- **Always On Availability Groups**:

- If using **SQL Server Enterprise Edition**, implement **Always On Availability Groups** for **high availability** and **disaster recovery**.

- Configure **automatic failover** to minimize downtime and ensure business continuity.

- **Database Mirroring/Log Shipping**:

  - For SQL Server Standard Edition or older versions, implement **database mirroring** or **log shipping** to ensure high availability.

  - Configure **backup** and **restore** strategies on secondary replicas for consistent replication.

- **Replication**:

  - Use **SQL Server transactional replication** to **distribute data** to multiple locations, improving data availability and performance.

  - Regularly monitor **replication health** and **error logs** to ensure smooth replication performance.

6. Security Best Practices

- **Authentication and Authorization**:

  - Use **Windows Authentication** over **SQL Server Authentication** for **increased security**.

  - Implement the **principle of least privilege** by granting users the minimum permissions necessary to perform their tasks.

  - **Roles and Permissions**: Assign users to **predefined roles** such as **db_datareader**, **db_datawriter**, and **db_owner** based on their responsibilities.

- **Encryption**:

  - Enable **Transparent Data Encryption (TDE)** for **encrypting data files at rest** to comply with security policies and regulations.

  - Use **Always Encrypted** to encrypt sensitive data, such as personally identifiable information (PII), in columns of SQL Server databases.

  - Implement **SSL/TLS** encryption for data in transit between SQL Server and applications.

- **Auditing**:

  - Implement **SQL Server Audit** to track login attempts, access to sensitive data, and changes to the database schema.

  - Store audit logs securely and regularly review logs for potential security threats.

7. Monitoring and Diagnostics

- **SQL Server Profiler and Extended Events**:

  - Use **SQL Server Profiler** or **Extended Events** to monitor and troubleshoot long-running queries, deadlocks, and resource bottlenecks.

  - Capture detailed logs and query execution data to **identify problematic queries** and **optimize them**.

- **Dynamic Management Views (DMVs)**:

  - Regularly query **DMVs** (such as sys.dm_exec_requests, sys.dm_exec_query_stats, and sys.dm_os_wait_stats) to analyze SQL Server performance and identify issues like blocking, long-running queries, and I/O waits.

Example:

sql

Copy

```
SELECT * FROM sys.dm_exec_requests;
```

- **Performance Baseline**:

  o Establish **performance baselines** by monitoring key metrics such as CPU usage, disk I/O, memory usage, and query performance during normal operation.

  o Regularly review these metrics to identify anomalies and plan for **capacity scaling**.

8. Scaling SQL Server for Growth

- **Vertical Scaling (Scaling Up)**:

- Increase server resources (CPU, RAM, disk space) when SQL Server's workload grows beyond current limits.

- Monitor **resource consumption** and **identify bottlenecks** to determine when it's time to scale up.

- **Horizontal Scaling (Scaling Out)**:

  - Implement **sharding** or **replication** strategies to distribute the workload across multiple servers or geographical locations for large-scale applications.

  - Consider **SQL Server on containers** or **Kubernetes** for **scalable, flexible cloud deployments**.

- **Cloud Integration**:

  - Migrate SQL Server databases to **cloud environments** such as **Azure SQL Database**, **AWS RDS**, or **Google Cloud SQL** for better scalability, high availability, and disaster recovery.

9. Disaster Recovery and Business Continuity

- **Disaster Recovery Plan**:

  - Develop and maintain a comprehensive **disaster recovery (DR) plan** to ensure SQL Server databases can be restored quickly in case of failure.

  - Test **failover** and **restore procedures** regularly.

- **Business Continuity**:

  - Ensure that all **critical SQL Server databases** have **replication** or **log shipping** in place to minimize downtime during unplanned outages.

  - Regularly test **disaster recovery scenarios** to validate that the plan works as expected.

10. Regular Database Maintenance

- **Index Maintenance**:

  - Regularly rebuild or reorganize indexes to ensure optimal performance.

o   Use **SQL Server Agent jobs** to automate index maintenance tasks.

- **Database Integrity Checks**:

    o   Perform regular **DBCC CHECKDB** commands to check for database corruption.

    o   Automate this process using **SQL Server Agent**.

- **Update Statistics**:

    o   Regularly update statistics to ensure that query optimization is based on the most accurate data.

    o   Schedule **automatic statistics updates** as needed.

Appendix B: Useful SQL Server Scripts and Commands

SQL Server DBAs and developers rely on a variety of **scripts and commands** to streamline routine database management tasks, perform advanced troubleshooting, and optimize SQL Server performance. This appendix provides a collection of the most **useful SQL Server scripts** and **commands** that can be employed to enhance productivity and maintain system health.

---

1. Basic SQL Server Commands

1.1. Checking SQL Server Version

To check the version and edition of SQL Server:

sql

Copy

```
SELECT @@VERSION;
```

1.2. Viewing All Databases

To list all databases in the SQL Server instance:

sql

Copy

```
SELECT name FROM sys.databases;
```

1.3. Viewing Current Server Configuration

To get details about the server's current configuration settings:

sql

Copy

```
EXEC sp_configure;
```

1.4. Viewing Active Connections

To find all active connections to SQL Server:

sql

Copy

```
SELECT session_id, login_name, host_name, program_name, status
FROM sys.dm_exec_sessions
```

```sql
WHERE is_user_process = 1;
```

---

2. Query and Performance Optimization

2.1. Viewing Query Execution Plans

To view the **execution plan** for a specific query:

sql

Copy

```sql
SET SHOWPLAN_ALL ON;

-- Your query here

SET SHOWPLAN_ALL OFF;
```

Alternatively, you can use:

sql

Copy

```sql
SET STATISTICS IO ON;

SET STATISTICS TIME ON;

-- Your query here

SET STATISTICS IO OFF;
```

SET STATISTICS TIME OFF;

2.2. Viewing Slow Running Queries

To identify slow-running queries, including execution times:

sql

Copy

```
SELECT TOP 10
    qs.total_elapsed_time / 1000.0 AS ElapsedTimeSeconds,
    qs.execution_count,
    qs.total_worker_time / 1000.0 AS CPUTimeSeconds,
    qs.total_logical_reads    /    qs.execution_count    AS
AvgLogicalReads,
    SUBSTRING(qt.text, qs.statement_start_offset / 2,
    (CASE
        WHEN qs.statement_end_offset = -1
        THEN LEN(CONVERT(NVARCHAR(MAX), qt.text))
* 2
```

```
    ELSE qs.statement_end_offset

    END - qs.statement_start_offset) / 2) AS QueryText

FROM

    sys.dm_exec_query_stats qs

CROSS APPLY

    sys.dm_exec_sql_text(qs.sql_handle) qt

ORDER BY

    ElapsedTimeSeconds DESC;
```

2.3. Checking Index Fragmentation

To check for index fragmentation:

sql

Copy

```
SELECT

    dbschemas.[name] AS SchemaName,

    dbobjects.[name] AS TableName,

    dbindexes.[name] AS IndexName,
```

```
    indexstats.avg_fragmentation_in_percent,

    indexstats.page_count

FROM

    sys.dm_db_index_physical_stats(DB_ID(), NULL, NULL,
NULL, 'DETAILED') indexstats

INNER JOIN

    sys.tables    dbobjects    ON    dbobjects.object_id    =
indexstats.object_id

INNER JOIN

    sys.schemas    dbschemas    ON    dbschemas.schema_id    =
dbobjects.schema_id

INNER JOIN

    sys.indexes    dbindexes    ON    dbindexes.object_id    =
dbobjects.object_id

WHERE

    indexstats.avg_fragmentation_in_percent > 30

    AND dbindexes.type_desc = 'CLUSTERED'

ORDER BY
```

indexstats.avg_fragmentation_in_percent DESC;

2.4. Rebuilding Fragmented Indexes

To rebuild fragmented indexes:

sql

Copy

```sql
ALTER INDEX [IndexName] ON [TableName] REBUILD;
```

To rebuild all indexes on a table:

sql

Copy

```sql
DECLARE @TableName NVARCHAR(128);

DECLARE @IndexName NVARCHAR(128);


DECLARE index_cursor CURSOR FOR

SELECT name, table_name

FROM sys.indexes

WHERE object_id = OBJECT_ID('[Schema].[TableName]');
```

```
OPEN index_cursor;

FETCH NEXT FROM index_cursor INTO @IndexName,
@TableName;


WHILE @@FETCH_STATUS = 0
BEGIN
   EXEC('ALTER INDEX [' + @IndexName + '] ON [' +
@TableName + '] REBUILD');

   FETCH NEXT FROM index_cursor INTO @IndexName,
@TableName;
END


CLOSE index_cursor;

DEALLOCATE index_cursor;
```

2.5. Creating Non-Clustered Indexes

To create a non-clustered index:

sql

Copy

CREATE NONCLUSTERED INDEX IX_ColumnName

ON TableName (ColumnName);

---

3. Backup and Recovery

3.1. Full Backup of a Database

To create a full backup of a database:

sql

Copy

BACKUP DATABASE [DatabaseName]

TO DISK = 'C:\Backups\DatabaseName.bak';

3.2. Transaction Log Backup

To back up the transaction log:

sql

Copy

```
BACKUP LOG [DatabaseName]

TO DISK = 'C:\Backups\DatabaseName_Log.bak';
```

3.3. Restoring a Database

To restore a full database backup:

sql

Copy

```
RESTORE DATABASE [DatabaseName]

FROM DISK = 'C:\Backups\DatabaseName.bak'

WITH RECOVERY;
```

To restore a transaction log backup:

sql

Copy

```
RESTORE LOG [DatabaseName]

FROM DISK = 'C:\Backups\DatabaseName_Log.bak'

WITH NORECOVERY;
```

3.4. Restoring a Database to a Point in Time

To restore a database to a point in time (useful for point-in-time recovery):

sql

Copy

```
RESTORE DATABASE [DatabaseName]

FROM DISK = 'C:\Backups\DatabaseName.bak'

WITH STOPAT = '2023-10-12T14:00:00';
```

---

4. High Availability and Disaster Recovery

4.1. Setting Up Always On Availability Groups

To configure Always On Availability Groups (on SQL Server Enterprise edition):

sql

Copy

-- Enable Always On feature on both primary and secondary instances:

ALTER AVAILABILITY GROUP [AGName]

ADD DATABASE [DatabaseName];

4.2. Checking Availability Group Health

To check the status of an Availability Group:

sql

Copy

```
SELECT
    ag.name AS AG_Name,
    replica_server_name AS Replica,
    ags.database_id,
    ags.database_name,
    ags.synchronization_state_desc,
    ags.synchronization_health_desc
FROM
```

sys.availability_groups ag

JOIN

sys.dm_hadr_availability_group_states ags

ON ag.group_id = ags.group_id;

4.3. Checking Database Mirroring Status

To monitor the database mirroring status:

sql

Copy

```
SELECT database_id, database_name, mirroring_guid,
state_desc
FROM sys.database_mirroring
WHERE database_id = DB_ID('YourDatabaseName');
```

---

5. Security Best Practices

5.1. Enabling Transparent Data Encryption (TDE)

To enable TDE (for encrypting the database at rest):

sql

Copy

```
CREATE DATABASE ENCRYPTION KEY;

CREATE DATABASE [DatabaseName]

SET ENCRYPTION ON;
```

5.2. Enabling Auditing

To enable auditing for login attempts and sensitive data access:

sql

Copy

```
CREATE SERVER AUDIT [AuditName]

TO FILE (FILEPATH = 'C:\AuditLogs\')

WITH (ON_FAILURE = CONTINUE);


CREATE SERVER AUDIT SPECIFICATION [AuditSpecName]

FOR SERVER AUDIT [AuditName]
```

ADD (FAILED_LOGIN_GROUP),

ADD (SUCCESSFUL_LOGIN_GROUP)

WITH (STATE = ON);

5.3. Granting Roles and Permissions

To grant a user a specific role:

sql

Copy

```
EXEC sp_addrolemember 'db_datareader', 'UserName';
```

To grant specific permissions:

sql

Copy

```
GRANT SELECT, INSERT, UPDATE ON TableName TO UserName;
```

---

6. Data Maintenance and Integrity

6.1. Database Integrity Check (DBCC CHECKDB)

To check the integrity of a database:

sql

Copy

DBCC CHECKDB ([DatabaseName]);

6.2. Updating Statistics

To update statistics for all tables in a database:

sql

Copy

EXEC sp_updatestats;

To update statistics for a specific table:

sql

Copy

UPDATE STATISTICS [TableName];

6.3. Rebuilding Indexes Regularly

To rebuild indexes in a database:

sql

Copy

```sql
EXEC sp_MSforeachtable 'ALTER INDEX ALL ON ? REBUILD';
```

---

7. Automating Tasks with SQL Server Agent Jobs

7.1. Creating a SQL Server Agent Job

To create a SQL Server Agent job to back up the database daily:

1. Right-click **SQL Server Agent** in SSMS > **New Job**.

2. Name the job and configure the **Steps** to run the backup command:

sql

Copy

```sql
BACKUP DATABASE [DatabaseName]

TO DISK = 'C:\Backups\DatabaseName.bak';
```

3. Set a **schedule** to run the job daily.

7.2. Job Alerts

To create an alert for a job failure:

sql

Copy

```sql
EXEC msdb.dbo.sp_add_alert
    @name = 'Job Failure Alert',
    @message_id = 22022,
    @severity = 16,
    @notification_message = 'A job has failed.',
    @enabled = 1;
```

---

8. Monitoring SQL Server Performance

8.1. Monitoring Query Execution

To view the active queries that are currently running:

sql

Copy

```sql
SELECT
```

```
    session_id,

    status,

    blocking_session_id,

    wait_type,

    wait_time,

    wait_resource,

    last_request_start_time,

    last_request_end_time,

    cpu_time,

    total_elapsed_time,

    text AS QueryText

FROM sys.dm_exec_requests

CROSS APPLY sys.dm_exec_sql_text(sql_handle)

WHERE session_id <> @@SPID;
```

8.2. Monitor System Waits

To monitor system waits, which help diagnose performance bottlenecks:

sql

Copy

```
SELECT wait_type, wait_time_ms, waiting_tasks_count

FROM sys.dm_os_wait_stats

WHERE wait_time_ms > 1000

ORDER BY wait_time_ms DESC;
```

Appendix C: Recommended Tools for SQL Server DBAs

SQL Server Database Administrators (DBAs) rely on a wide variety of tools to manage, monitor, and optimize SQL Server instances. These tools can help improve productivity, automate routine tasks, troubleshoot performance issues, ensure security, and maintain high availability. In this appendix, we will explore **essential tools** for SQL Server DBAs, categorized into **management tools**, **performance monitoring tools**, **backup and recovery tools**, **security tools**, and **third-party tools** that provide added functionality and efficiency.

---

1. SQL Server Management Tools

1.1. SQL Server Management Studio (SSMS)

SQL Server Management Studio (SSMS) is the primary tool used by DBAs for managing and configuring SQL Server instances. It provides a user-friendly interface for tasks such as query execution, database configuration, performance monitoring, and security management.

Key Features:

- **Query editor** for writing and executing SQL queries.

- **Object Explorer** for navigating SQL Server instances, databases, tables, views, and other objects.

- **SQL Profiler** for capturing and analyzing SQL Server events.

- **Backup and restore management**.

- **Integrated solutions for database tuning and optimization**.

Why DBAs Should Use SSMS:

- **Comprehensive** toolset for most database administration tasks.

- **Free** and fully supported by Microsoft for SQL Server management.

1.2. Azure Data Studio

Azure Data Studio is a cross-platform database management tool that works on **Windows, macOS**, and **Linux**. It is often seen as a modern alternative to SSMS with an emphasis on **query editing, notebooks**, and **visualization**.

Key Features:

- Supports both **SQL Server** and **Azure SQL Database**.

- Includes **IntelliSense**, **code snippets**, and **source control** integration.

- Offers a **notebook** interface for combining code and results, ideal for data science and ad-hoc reporting.

- Supports **PowerShell** and **SQL notebooks** for automation.

Why DBAs Should Use Azure Data Studio:

- Ideal for **cloud-first environments** and those working with both **SQL Server** and **Azure SQL**.

- Offers **more modern workflows** and integrations for users who prefer **cross-platform** management.

---

2. Performance Monitoring and Diagnostic Tools

2.1. SQL Profiler

SQL Profiler is a built-in tool in SSMS that captures real-time events from a SQL Server instance, providing valuable information about query performance, errors, and deadlocks.

Key Features:

- Monitors **SQL Server events**, such as queries, stored procedures, and error events.

- Records **execution times, CPU usage**, and **I/O statistics**.

- Supports **deadlock graph capture** and **query execution plan analysis**.

- Can export captured data to a file for further analysis.

Why DBAs Should Use SQL Profiler:

- Ideal for **troubleshooting performance problems** and understanding **query-level behavior**.

- Useful for diagnosing **deadlocks** and **query plan inefficiencies**.

2.2. Extended Events

Extended Events is a lightweight and powerful tool used for **tracing** and **diagnosing SQL Server issues**. It is designed to replace SQL Profiler, offering lower overhead and greater flexibility for capturing performance data.

Key Features:

- Provides highly granular data capture for SQL Server events.

- Allows DBAs to create custom event sessions and filters.

- Supports **real-time monitoring** and **event streaming**.

- Allows storage of data in **ring buffers** or **files** for later analysis.

Why DBAs Should Use Extended Events:

- Essential for **high-performance environments** where **minimal overhead** is critical.

- Offers more **flexible and scalable** event tracking than SQL Profiler.

2.3. Performance Monitor (PerfMon)

Performance Monitor is a built-in Windows tool that enables DBAs to monitor system performance in real-time, including **CPU**, **memory**, **disk**, and **network usage**.

Key Features:

- Tracks **SQL Server performance counters**, such as **buffer cache hit ratio** and **SQL Statistics**.

- Offers **customizable charts** to monitor system resources.

- Supports the creation of **data collector sets** for continuous monitoring.

Why DBAs Should Use Performance Monitor:

- Ideal for monitoring **system resources** to identify performance bottlenecks.

- Allows **detailed tracking** of key metrics over time to diagnose issues.

2.4. DMVs (Dynamic Management Views)

Dynamic Management Views (DMVs) provide DBAs with real-time insights into SQL Server's internal state, including performance metrics, locking and blocking, index usage, and more.

Key Features:

- Provides **real-time monitoring** of SQL Server's internal components.

- Allows you to query and analyze **query performance, wait stats**, and **index fragmentation**.

- Helps diagnose **blocking issues, deadlocks**, and **slow queries**.

Why DBAs Should Use DMVs:

- Provides a powerful method for **diagnosing issues** using SQL queries.

- **No extra tools** required — just SQL Server's built-in capabilities.

---

3. Backup and Recovery Tools

3.1. Redgate SQL Backup

Redgate SQL Backup is a third-party tool that enhances the backup and restore functionality of SQL Server. It provides **advanced compression** and **scheduling** features that improve backup performance and ease of management.

Key Features:

- **High compression** to reduce backup size and storage requirements.

- **Flexible scheduling** and **automated backups**.

- **Backup verification** to ensure integrity.

- **Point-in-time restores** and **transaction log backups**.

Why DBAs Should Use Redgate SQL Backup:

- **Improves backup speed** and storage efficiency, reducing downtime.

- Ideal for **large databases** and **high-volume environments**.

3.2. Idera SQL Safe Backup

Idera SQL Safe Backup is another third-party backup tool designed to enhance SQL Server's backup and restore operations. It offers **high-performance backup** and **disaster recovery** features.

Key Features:

- Supports **disk-based backups** with **compression** and **encryption**.

- **Backup verification** and **restore testing**.

- **Centralized backup management** for multiple SQL Server instances.

- **Deduplication** to save space.

Why DBAs Should Use Idera SQL Safe Backup:

- **Fast backups** with **minimal impact** on SQL Server performance.

- **Centralized management** makes it easy to manage backups across multiple servers.

---

4. Security Tools

4.1. SQL Server Audit

SQL Server's built-in **SQL Server Audit** feature allows DBAs to track and log **database activity**, including login events, schema changes, and data access.

Key Features:

- **Real-time auditing** of sensitive data and user actions.

- Supports **granular filtering** of events (e.g., specific tables, actions).

- **Compliance reporting** for regulatory standards such as PCI-DSS and HIPAA.

Why DBAs Should Use SQL Server Audit:

- Essential for ensuring **data security** and **regulatory compliance**.

- Provides detailed logs for auditing and forensic analysis.

4.2. ApexSQL Security

ApexSQL Security is a comprehensive third-party tool that focuses on **SQL Server security auditing** and **vulnerability assessments**.

Key Features:

- Provides detailed **security audits** of SQL Server instances.

- Identifies **permissions vulnerabilities**, such as excessive privileges or SQL injection risks.

- Tracks **user activity** and **changes to sensitive data**.

Why DBAs Should Use ApexSQL Security:

- Offers detailed **security analysis** and helps **identify vulnerabilities**.

- Helps **audit user activity** and changes to **confidential data**.

---

5. Third-Party Tools for Extended Functionality

5.1. Redgate SQL Monitor

Redgate SQL Monitor is a third-party tool that provides a **web-based dashboard** for monitoring SQL Server performance across multiple instances. It gives DBAs detailed insights into **health, availability,** and **performance metrics**.

Key Features:

- **Real-time monitoring** of SQL Server instances and databases.

- **Alerts and notifications** for critical performance issues.

- **Historical trend analysis** for resource usage, query performance, and more.

Why DBAs Should Use Redgate SQL Monitor:

- Provides a **centralized monitoring dashboard** for SQL Server instances.

- Helps **proactively manage performance** and **reduce downtime**.

5.2. SolarWinds Database Performance Analyzer (DPA)

SolarWinds DPA is a comprehensive performance monitoring tool that helps DBAs diagnose and optimize **SQL Server performance**.

Key Features:

- **Database performance analysis** with detailed insights into query performance, wait times, and more.

- **Root cause analysis** to identify bottlenecks and optimize queries.

- Integration with **SQL Server Profiler** for deeper diagnostics.

Why DBAs Should Use SolarWinds DPA:

- **Comprehensive performance tuning** and **root cause analysis** tools.

- Helps identify **inefficient queries** and **bottlenecks** that affect SQL Server performance.

5.3. dbForge Studio for SQL Server

dbForge Studio for SQL Server is a versatile IDE (Integrated Development Environment) that provides DBAs and

developers with a range of tools for **query building,
performance monitoring**, and **database management**.

Key Features:

- **Visual query builder** and **SQL editor** with **IntelliSense** support.

- **Database design tools** for building, managing, and migrating databases.

- **Schema and data comparison** for version control and data migrations.

Why DBAs Should Use dbForge Studio:

- Great for **SQL development, debugging,** and **database management** in a single interface.

- Ideal for **performance optimization** with visual tools and **query building** capabilities.

www.ingramcontent.com/pod-product-compliance
Lightning Source LLC
Chambersburg PA
CBHW071105050326
40690CB00008B/1122